JEREMIAH
A FRESH READING

JEREMIAH
A FRESH READING

WILLIAM L. HOLLADAY

THE PILGRIM PRESS
NEW YORK

Scripture quotations from the Revised Standard Version of the Bible, copyrighted 1946, 1952, © 1971, 1973 by the Division of Christian Education of the National Council of the Churches of Christ in the U.S.A. are used by permission. Scripture quotations from the New Revised Standard Version Bible, copyright 1989, Division of Christian Education of the National Council of the Churches of Christ in the United States of America are used by permission. Excerpts from *Jeremiah 2* copyright © Fortress Press are used by permission of Augsburg Fortress.

Design by Publishers' WorkGroup

Library of Congress Cataloging-in-Publication Data

Holladay, William Lee.
    Jeremiah : a fresh reading / William L. Holladay.
        p.   cm.
    Includes index.
    ISBN 0–8298–0848–5
    1. Bible. O.T. Jeremiah—Criticism, interpretation, etc.
2. Bible. O.T. Jeremiah—Chronology. 3. Jeremiah (Biblical prophet)—Chronology. I. Title.
BS1525.2.H638   1990
224'.2—dc20   90–31891
                                                              CIP

The Pilgrim Press, 475 Riverside Drive, New York, NY 10115

CONTENTS

FOREWORD

The parentage of this book is complicated. Its grandmother was three lectures I was invited to give near Istanbul in the spring of 1966 for members of the Near East Mission of the United Church Board for World Ministries, lectures that were later privately printed by the mission.[1] I am grateful that this invitation led me for the first time to try to write down in nontechnical form what seems crucial about Jeremiah.

Its mother was *Jeremiah: Spokesman Out of Time* (New York: Pilgrim Press, 1974). In that book the three lectures of 1966 became ten chapters, a study guide for pastors and lay groups in churches on the prophet Jeremiah. Then in 1976 I began the preparation of what has turned out to be the father of this book, the two volumes on Jeremiah in the Hermeneia commentary series, *Jeremiah 1* (Philadelphia: Fortress Press, 1986) and *Jeremiah 2* (Minneapolis: Augsburg Fortress, 1989).

In the course of preparing that work I came to the conclusion that an attempt should be made to sort out Jeremiah's various utterances chronologically and to hear them as closely as possible in the context of the events of their time. This is a risky business, as I shall indicate in more detail in a moment. However, the conclusions I reached in the course of working on the two-volume commentary have rendered the material in *Jeremiah: Spokesman Out of Time* less than satisfactory for me, and I have been urged to revise it.

As I embarked upon a revision, however, it became clear that a simple revision would not do. This book, then, is a new work. Because it is a new work, it has a new title, and because the reconstruction of Jeremiah's life and work in the book is my own rather than one shared by other scholars generally, I have chosen the title *Jeremiah: A Fresh Reading*.

But if this book is shaped by the conclusions of *Jeremiah 1* and *Jeremiah 2*, the extensive commentary, its purpose is still that of *Jeremiah: Spokesman Out of Time*: to offer to students and lay groups in churches, who may have little background in biblical matters, some understanding of one of the most remarkable figures in Scripture.

This is a new work, yes; but the fact that it has a complicated history means that at a few points it shares wording with its antecedents. In the first chapter, in the last chapter, and in my treatment of such passages as Jer. 31:31–34 (the "new covenant" passage), I have sometimes followed the wording of one of my antecedent works.

I have made every effort to keep my presentation of Jeremiah straightforward and clear; nevertheless, the material will often betray that habit of the professor, namely, raising questions. There may be more questions here, more doubts, more uncertainties than many readers will feel comfortable with—particularly in the last chapter, where I try to give a fair presentation of what the story of Jeremiah can mean to us today. I can only say that to my mind raising questions about Scripture is not a wicked thing to do. Indeed, Scripture itself implies questions as the careful reader begins to notice contrasts, differences of perspective, and other curiosities within its pages. Many generations within the Jewish and Christian communities have raised such questions. In the meantime, Scripture has survived—and thrived. And it will survive and thrive on our questions, too. As we raise our own questions and discover our own answers, our eyes will be sharpened, and the biblical story will emerge in clearer focus for us.

On the other hand, if some general readers find more doubts and questions in these pages than they are comfortable with, other readers with some acquaintance with the course of research on Jeremiah will find in these pages more certainties than they are comfortable with. This brings me back to the "risky business" of which I have already spoken, my attempt to bring some kind of chronological order to the utterances of Jeremiah.

Two things are clear. First, the book of Jeremiah is by and large not arranged chronologically. Second, there are far too few clues in the book of Jeremiah for any certitude in the matter of framing a chronology of the prophet's career. The book of Jeremiah took shape in many stages, and there is at present no agreement among scholars as to how to reconstruct these stages. What we have before us is evidently many small collections of sayings of the prophet and recollections about him, collections and recollections that were gathered over a period of many years. The collectors of this material were more interested in getting them all and saving them than in putting them in any kind of chronological sequence. The result is a crazy quilt. The reader who wants to understand the passages of the book in the light of the events of the time or in the light of other passages in the book from the same period faces great difficulties.

In my commentary in the Hermeneia series I attempt to sort out these problems and offer solutions, and it is a synthesis of these solutions that I offer here. But *that very attempt to sort out the chronological problems* is one of the chief criticisms that reviewers have made of my commentary, and this book is thus open to the same criticism: there are scholars who are convinced that no chronology of the prophet is possible. I see no way out of the problem: this is the way I see Jeremiah! My view is at least a consistent one and, further, one that I believe brings the prophet to life in a plausible way. But readers must continually understand that this is my own reconstruction, that other ways to understand the book of Jeremiah are possible, and that truer ones may yet be found. Those who wish to explore my solutions in more detail and to learn more about alternative views are urged to consult the larger commentary, where full bibliographical resources are to be found. I simply reaffirm here what I stated in the foreword to *Jeremiah: Spokesman Out of Time:* It is only fair to warn the reader that not all scholars would agree with everything presented here. I have tried my best, however, to be responsible in my presentation.

I urge that this book be read not as a substitute for reading and studying the Old Testament book of Jeremiah but rather as a companion to it. I do not quote all the relevant Old Testament material; usually I simply comment on the text and give some of the background and illustrative material that I hope will illuminate the text. When I discuss it, a chapter-and-verse citation should be looked up and read.

For simplicity's sake all references to a chapter (or chapter and verse) in Arabic numerals, unaccompanied by any book reference, are citations to a particular passage in the book of Jeremiah (and of course to the English verse references rather than to the Hebrew ones, when these differ). Cross-references to other chapters *within this volume* are in Roman numerals. When a phrase or a passage is quoted in this study, it is, unless otherwise noted, from the New Revised Standard Version (NRSV), published in 1990. I should like to express my appreciation to the Division of Education and Ministry of the National Council of the Churches of Christ in the United States of America for permission to make advance use of that translation of the book of Jeremiah.

As I have already indicated, readers will have to jump around a lot in the book of Jeremiah to locate and compare passages that, by my judgment, need to be seen together. There is no help for this. I only hope that the sense of the forward movement in the narrative of Jeremiah's life will compensate for the necessity of jumping around. To help in this I have included an index to Scripture passages.

There are two additional scholarly matters that I need to touch on here. The first is that most of the utterances of Jeremiah were probably short, typically six or eight or ten verses in length. By contrast, our Bible offers long chapters of material. What needs to be done, then, is to locate the *boundaries* of a given utterance of the prophet. Recent translations of the Bible try to do this (the Revised Standard Version [RSV] and the New Revised Standard Version [NRSV] by "white spaces," for example, after 2:3, 8, 13, etc.). But scholars do not always agree about where these boundaries are. Thus, one more uncertainty.

The second is that Jeremiah is one of the books of the Old Testament that has had a long and complicated *textual* history. That is, the very wording of the original Hebrew is often open to question, in particular because the Septuagint, an early translation into Greek from the Hebrew text made about 200 B.C.E., often gives a rather different wording, suggesting that the book of Jeremiah was still undergoing changes and expansion four hundred years after the prophet's death. Sometimes the Septuagint is useful in clarifying the original wording, and I refer to it from time to time.

Once again I should like to express my thanks to all those thoughtful folk through the years—in the Chicago area in 1960–63, in Lebanon and Turkey in 1963–70, and in New England since 1970—who have had a hand in this book by teaching me through their questions and their responses what is really important to the book of Jeremiah. This study is offered, then, to church and classroom in the hope that it can stimulate discussion and further exploration, not only of Jeremiah but of other portions of Scripture as well. Pastor John Robinson's parting words to the Pilgrim Fathers in 1620 are appropriate here: a friend recalled, "For he was very confident the Lord had more truth and light yet to break forth out of his holy Word."[2]

NOTES

1. The lectures (called simply *Jeremiah*) were privately printed by the American Mission Press, Istanbul, 1966.

2. *The Works of John Robinson, with a Memoir and Annotations by Robert Ashton* (London: John Snow, 1851), I:xliv.

JEREMIAH
A FRESH READING

JEREMIAH AND HIS WORLD

A French scholar has recently written, "Prophetism taken as a whole constitutes a sort of backbone of the Old Testament. . . . Now the prophet par excellence, the one who can allow us to surmise to some degree the experience lived by those men and their role in history, is indisputably Jeremiah."[1]

Yet while Jeremiah is a kind of model for our understanding of the prophets of the Old Testament, church people have not always had easy access to him. For much of Christian history the churches have looked upon the books of the prophets as sources for the Christian story, and of course the book of Isaiah has figured chiefly in that endeavor (as the Christmas carol "Lo, how a rose e'er blooming" says, "Isaiah 'twas foretold it"). Thus, in the selection of Old Testament passages in the Roman Catholic lectionary of daily and weekly readings, there are few from the book of Jeremiah, and those that are used do not bring the prophet into focus. Bible readers who undertake to read the book of Jeremiah from beginning to end find sections of poetry alternating with sections of prose, almost all of them full of anticipations of destruction and death, with little apparent coherent organization (see my remarks in the Foreword). It is no wonder that the prophet Jeremiah remains for most Christians a distant and fuzzy figure.

Yet Jeremiah is an exceptional figure in the biblical record in terms of both the extent of his own words that are recorded and the amount of biographical information recorded about him. His own words—mainly in the form of "oracles," short poetic units announcing God's judgment or restoration, but some sermons as well—appear in chapters 2—23, 30—31, and 46—51. The biographical information about him appears in chapters 26—29 and 32—44. While there is more biographical information about King David in the Old Testament and more recorded words from the apostle Paul in the New, nevertheless in the extent of both recorded words and biographical information in the Bible, Jeremiah would be difficult to match.

Moreover, we have more than just a record of many of his words and deeds; those words and deeds give every evidence of his being a highly unique person who anticipated and witnessed the turning point in the history of the people of the Old Testament. That turning point, in 587 B.C.E., was the fall of Jerusalem, the capital of the kingdom of Judah, to Nebuchadrezzar, the king of the great empire of Babylon. (We commonly know this king as Nebuchadnezzar, with an *n*, but the Bible spells it both ways; cf. 29:1, 21. The spelling with an *r* is closer to the Babylonian pronunciation.) Jeremiah's ministry was lived out in the last few decades of that kingdom of Judah and for a year or so after the fall of Jerusalem.

Jeremiah was convinced that his mission was to announce to his people God's judgment upon them for their disloyalty, a judgment manifested primarily through an invasion and defeat by the Babylonian army. Because the Babylonian army did invade, and Judah did fall, Jeremiah was largely responsible for shaping a theology adequate for the disaster that overwhelmed the people. And because there was no alternative theology available that had the adequacy Jeremiah's did, it was his outlook which helped to shape the people's view of itself during those terrible years of defeat and humiliation and, indeed, for the half century following his death when the people were forced to reconceive their destiny through and through.

All of this should suffice to alert us to Jeremiah's importance in biblical history. And since we in our own century are witnesses to both triumph and disaster in human fortune that seem to us almost unmatched, we may find clues in Jeremiah's testimony for an appropriate response to the issues of our own time.

Jeremiah—The Questioning Prophet

But there is even more to Jeremiah that attracts many in our own generation to him. Alone of the "prophets" of the Old Testament, he saw his relationship with God to be a problem to be grappled with, more than simply an obligation to be taken for granted. There had been other prophets who spoke for God, great ones, in times past—Elijah and Amos, Hosea and Micah and Isaiah. But one finds, in reading through the pages that record their words and deeds, that once they became convinced that God was calling them to speak, they spoke, and that was that; so far as our record goes, no question crossed their minds regarding the nature of their calling.

Jeremiah, however, while he went ahead and spoke, nonetheless hesitated before accepting the task and continued to question the way God was treating him. In his capacity and willingness to question and to doubt, he stands out from most of the people found in the pages of Scripture; and this capacity and willingness bring him close to us. For while there are many people in our day who are willing to undertake a life of faith lived under God's guidance and care, there are few who do not at some point question God's ways—or wish they dared to.

Time and Place

We must begin by taking some account of the world in which Jeremiah lived. For a point in time, we shall say 627 B.C.E. For locale, of course, we turn to Palestine.

I use the word "Palestine" as a geographical term, not a political one, to refer to the area at the eastern end of the Mediterranean Sea, where the people of the Old Testament lived out their destiny and their faith. It is a surprisingly small area, not much larger than the states of New Hampshire or Vermont, about ten thousand square miles. Within this area are several spots suitable for large-scale farming, notably on the coast and in the valley of Jezreel (Esdraelon) in the north. Most of the region, however, is cut up by hills and dry stream beds (very much like the arroyos of the American Southwest) and is made suitable for agriculture only by the patient terracing of hillsides. Those who are familiar with the way the land looks east of Santa Barbara or San Diego can form some idea of the terrain, though those areas of California receive less rainfall than Palestine does.

Palestine may receive more rain than does southern California, but the pattern of rainy and dry seasons is much the same. The rainy season begins late in October and rain falls intermittently until March or April. The dry season lasts through the summer and early fall. The amount of rain varies from north to south and from west to east, the areas in the north and west getting the most. Little rain reaches beyond the hills west of the Jordan River. Jerusalem receives about twenty-four inches of rain per year.

Into this area, which acts as a land bridge between Egypt and Assyria and Babylon, the two great civilizations of the east, there came, in the course of the thirteenth century B.C.E., a people with a fresh sense of community, the people called Israel. Their sense of community was shaped by a new vision, a new understanding of God. They were convinced that God had appeared to Moses, had revealed to Moses the name by which the people were to know God—"Yahweh"—and had then "covenanted," or contracted, with them, under the guidance of Moses. This covenanting, or contracting, had taken place at the mountain of Sinai. The covenant bound Yahweh and Israel together; Israel was to be "Yahweh's people," and Yahweh was to be "their God." Yahweh would protect them in war and prosper them in peace. The people, for their part, were to be a demonstration community, regulating their lives by mutual support and concern for the helpless and by continuing to be sensitive to Yahweh's will. For many decades this people worked out the patterns of their common life on the basis of these traditions from Sinai and reaffirmed their mutual loyalty to Yahweh at religious centers like Shiloh, where the Ark of the Covenant—a kind of box or chest which represented the presence of Yahweh with them—was kept.

But in the course of time new pressures came, principally the military threat of the Philistines, another group of people who had also settled in Palestine, on its southern coast (in the area now called the Gaza Strip). Israel found itself, late in the eleventh century B.C.E., forced to set up the institution of kingship for the sake of tighter and more secure government. This kingship began with Saul and prospered under David and Solomon but then, in 922 B.C.E., split into a northern kingdom and a southern one. While the people never lost their sense of united "peoplehood" under Yahweh, the two kingdoms were never reunited. The northern kingdom was called Israel (confusingly, for us, since that term was also applied to the totality of the people, north and south), and its capital was ultimately at Samaria. The southern kingdom was called Judah, and it continued the capital of David and Solomon at Jerusalem. All of Palestine was roughly the size of New Hampshire; Judah, very much the smaller of the two kingdoms, was scarcely larger than Rhode Island. Our story will center on Judah.

Before turning to Judah, however, we must take account of the great empires that surrounded it. There was Egypt, of course, to the southwest. Egypt's power had continued with few interruptions for more than two thousand years. Many times Egypt had extended its power by military or commercial activity in Palestine. There is a vivid description in 1 Kings 14:25–28 of the invasion of Palestine by the Pharaoh Shishak in 918 B.C.E. But in the centuries that followed, Egypt had left Palestine alone. Indeed, in 671 B.C.E. and for a decade thereafter, Egypt was unable to defend itself against invasions by the Assyrian army.

Assyria was the great military threat in the period just before Jeremiah's time. Assyria had its capital at various locations on the upper Tigris River, far to the east of Palestine; the final capital, Nineveh, was located where the city of Mosul is today, in northern Iraq, about six hundred miles northeast of Jerusalem. Its armies were the horror of the Middle East; for two or three hundred years they had spread out from the center of their empire to all points of the compass, killing and burning, ruling by deportation and terror. Perhaps not until the coming of the Mongols, in the thirteenth century C.E., did the people of the area so greatly fear and hate another conqueror. (We can glimpse the hatred the Jews held for the Assyrians by reading, in Nahum 1:12—3:14, the gloating account they framed when Nineveh finally, finally was falling.)

In 722 B.C.E., a hundred years before the time of Jeremiah, the Assyrians had marched into Palestine and besieged Samaria, the capital of the northern kingdom, until it fell. Isaiah, a prophet in the south, in Jerusalem, warned his people from Jerusalem about what was happening. Two decades later, in 701 B.C.E., the Assyrians returned and marched to the very gates of Jerusalem; and this time Isaiah actually watched the siege. The vivid account in 2

Kings 18:13—19:4 gives some notion of the fear the Assyrian general instilled in the inhabitants of Jerusalem. After some time, to the surprise of most people but in fulfillment of Isaiah's assurances (2 Kings 19:7), the Assyrian army suddenly pulled up stakes and marched home again.

But the threat of the Assyrian empire lay heavy on Judah in the years that followed. The long reign of King Manasseh of Judah (687–642 B.C.E.) was filled with frantic attempts to keep the nation intact, to assure its survival on any terms. And Judah did survive, barely, by becoming a puppet kingdom, a satellite of Assyria, by paying heavy tribute ("protection money") year after year to Assyria, by erecting Assyrian altars in the Temple area of Jerusalem, by cultivating astrology and fortunetelling in the Assyrian fashion—anything to assure Assyria of Judah's loyalty, anything to survive.

After King Manasseh's death and following the two-year reign of his son, Amon, the boy-king Josiah came to the throne. By the time Josiah reached adulthood, it was plain that he brought a great deal more sensitivity to religious issues than his grandfather Manasseh had. And, by 627 B.C.E., when we begin our story, something else was plain, too: Assyria was becoming weaker. The feeling in Judah was that Assyria was starting to rot from within, that its policy of ruling by terror was beginning to be counterproductive, and that it was beginning to be safe for its subject people to show a little independence. In short, people sensed that new policies were possible.

And they were correct. By 612 B.C.E. Assyrian power would shrink to nothing, for Assyria would be defeated by its southern rival, Babylon. Babylon was a great city on the Euphrates River, fifty miles south of the present city of Baghdad, the capital of Iraq, and thus about 280 miles south and a little east of Nineveh. Babylon and Assyria shared a common culture and language, but the two centers had always been rivals. In fact, for over a thousand years in the region of the Tigris and Euphrates Rivers, the question had been whether the north (Assyria) would rule over the south or the south (Babylon) would rule over the north. Assyria's fall was welcome news in Jerusalem. Few people in Judah imagined that in but a few years Babylon would assume Assyria's imperial designs and pursue them with equal vigor, a pursuit that would end, as noted earlier, with Nebuchadrezzar's capture and destruction of Jerusalem in 587 B.C.E.

In this period, when the foundations of international life were being shaken, Jeremiah was growing up.

I have said nothing in detail about the religious convictions of the Israelites, about what they believed about creation and redemption and human destiny, nor anything, for that matter, about the way in which they organized their religious observance. I will refer to some of these matters in the course of our exploration of the words and deeds of Jeremiah. But we must plunge into our central concern, and so we turn to chapter 1 of the book of Jeremiah, which records the prophet's perception of being called by Yahweh to speak out.

NOTES

1. André Ridouard, *Jérémie, l'épreuve de la foi* (Paris: Cerf, 1983), 7.

THE PROPHET LIKE MOSES

Chapter 1 of the book of Jeremiah opens with three verses that are heavy with information, enough to put off even the bravest reader! But it is important to persevere, for the verses are a kind of abbreviated introduction placed here to give us the immediate situation of Jeremiah's career.

A Historical Introduction

To those who lived nearer the times and places of the events, v. 1 was replete with details that set the stage. "The words of Jeremiah, the son of Hilkiah, of the priests who were in Anathoth in the land of Benjamin. . . ." The site of Anathoth, Jeremiah's village, is just three miles northeast of Jerusalem; the spot is a rocky prominence that local Arabs today call "Summit of Carob-beans." Memories are long in the Middle East, and the present-day Arab village just north of this spot carries the same name as Jeremiah's village: in Arabic, 'Anata. From the hillock where Jeremiah grew up, one may today clearly see the northern suburbs of Jerusalem. The boy grew up, then, not *in* the great capital city but within reach of it.

His father, Hilkiah, was a priest and so would have presided at the sacrifices of the villagers at Anathoth. In these days, before King Josiah's great reform, sacrifices were widespread. After the reform, sacrifices would be allowed only at the Temple in Jerusalem.

The priests had another function in those days, too: they had the responsibility of preserving and handing on the old traditions of instruction in covenant norms—how the community of Israel was expected to behave in the sight of Yahweh. This instruction was called *tōrāh:* not quite "law" in our sense (that would be a development of later times) but teaching, instruction in the stipulations that Yahweh had made to Israel about the conduct of life. The priests, then, were charged with the responsibility for the old testimony of Israel.

Jeremiah, then, would have absorbed directly from his father Hilkiah the religious traditions of early Israel. These traditions were likely to be the specific ones that had once resided in the old sanctuary at Shiloh. Shiloh was located twenty miles north of Anathoth, and there, centuries before, was the place where the Ark of the Covenant was kept. The Ark of the Covenant was a symbol of the presence of Yahweh, particularly during the Israelites' wanderings in the wilderness under Moses' leadership.[1] Shiloh was likewise the sanctuary where the boy Samuel grew up under the care of the priest Eli. Jeremiah is one of the few prophets to mention Moses and the only prophet to mention Samuel (15:1; the passage is discussed in chap. VII), and he is the only prophet to mention Shiloh (7:12; 26:6; see chap. III). A likely historical link between Shiloh and Anathoth is this: King Solomon deposed the priest Abiathar and ordered him to retire to Anathoth (1 Kings 2:26), and that same Abiathar is reported to have been the last survivor of the house of Eli the priest.[2] In any event, Jeremiah had a rich store of tradition from which to draw.

The second verse of chapter 1 gives us an important chronological clue: "to whom the word of the Lord came in the days of Josiah the son of Amon, king of Judah, in the thirteenth year of his reign." Data elsewhere in the Old Testament indicate that Josiah took the throne in 640 B.C.E., so that the thirteenth year of his reign would be 627 B.C.E.: this is the reference year for the description of the historical situation mentioned in chapter I. Now what precisely happened to Jeremiah in 627 B.C.E.? To decide, we must have a preliminary look at the description that has come down to us of Jeremiah's call (vv. 4–10).

> Now the word of the Lord came to me saying,
> "Before I formed you in the womb I knew you,
> and before you were born I consecrated you;
> I appointed you a prophet to the nations."
> Then I said, "Ah, Lord God! Behold, I do not know how to speak,
> for I am only a youth." But the Lord said to me,

"Do not say, 'I am only a youth';
for to all to whom I send you you shall go,
and whatever I command you you shall speak.
Be not afraid of them,
for I am with you to deliver you,
   says the Lord."
Then the Lord put forth his hand and touched my mouth; and the
   Lord said to me,
"Behold, I have put my words in your mouth.
See, I have set you this day over nations and over kingdoms,
to pluck up and to break down,
to destroy and to overthrow,
to build and to plant."

This is a portrayal of a reluctant prophet. Yahweh, we are told, called Jeremiah, and Jeremiah tried to beg off; but Yahweh overruled Jeremiah's hesitation and assured him that he would be protected by Yahweh in all that he undertook on Yahweh's behalf. Before I can continue to discuss the matter of Jeremiah's hesitation, I must first try to settle the matter of chronology, a tedious, but necessary, issue in this quest to put Jeremiah into focus.

Commentators have almost unanimously assumed without question that 627 B.C.E. is the date marking the beginning of Jeremiah's career as a prophet. In this view, Jeremiah began to speak out God's words to his fellow citizens in that year.[3] However, I find five problems in this view.

1. We find no oracles of Jeremiah that can be assigned with any confidence to the years just after 627 B.C.E.
2. In particular, there is no word from Jeremiah about the great reform of King Josiah in 622 B.C.E.
3. There is no good candidate in that period of time for the "foe from the north" about whom Jeremiah spoke so often (4:6–7; 5:15–17; 6:22–23).
4. The curious phrasing of 15:16 suggests that Jeremiah accepted his call *after* the finding of the scroll in the Temple in 622 B.C.E. and therefore not in 627 B.C.E.
5. Jeremiah declared his celibacy at a particular point in his career (16:1–4), by my analysis in 601 B.C.E. If 627 B.C.E. had been the year when he accepted his call, he would appear to be too old when he declared his celibacy.

These difficulties in the traditional chronology force upon us what I think is a simple solution that brings with it a clearer and more plausible picture of Jeremiah's self-understanding than we have had. I shall take up the first three of these problems now, discuss the fourth later in this chapter, and discuss the fifth in chapter VII.

The Absence of Oracles

We find no oracles of Jeremiah that can confidently be assigned to the years in Josiah's reign immediately after 627 B.C.E. This is negative evidence, of course, but worrisome nonetheless. The conventional view of Josiah found in 2 Kings 23:25 is that he was a good and excellent king, beyond compare. And while Jeremiah could conceivably have differed to some degree from this judgment, the single reference we have from him about Josiah is thoroughly positive. See 22:15–16, a passage that offers Jeremiah's negative judgment of King Jehoiakim in comparison with his father Josiah (read all of 22:13–19). It is probable that the oracles that appear in the beginning of the book of Jeremiah (in chaps. 2–10) were necessarily the earliest he delivered.

The main thrust of these oracles, as I will discuss in chapter IV, is that Israel has gone radically astray, has broken the covenant with Yahweh, and has been "harlotrous" with fertility deities. Consequently Yahweh is about to launch a fearful enemy from the north to lay waste and destroy the land and people of Israel. This overwhelmingly bleak picture simply does not seem to fit the situation of King Josiah's time. Josiah had hoped to reestablish his sovereignty over the lost territories of the north; according to 2 Chronicles 34 he began a religious-political reform as early as 628 B.C.E., his twelfth year (and the year before our date of 627!), smashing the (presumably pagan) altars in the north (2 Chron. 34:3–7). As we shall see, he undertook a thoroughgoing reform in Jerusalem in 622.

Moreover, there are no oracles elsewhere in the book of Jeremiah that seem to fit the circumstances of these years. All of the presumably early oracles of Jeremiah fit far better into the historical situation of the reign of Jehoiakim, son of Josiah. There are, it is true, traces of oracles Jeremiah delivered just before Josiah's death in 609 B.C.E. that seem to have been directed to the north (e.g.,

3:12–14; 31:4–6), but this material directed to the north was re-shaped for and delivered to a southern audience in Judah years later, and it is in their southern shape that we will study them in chapter X. Thus nothing that we know from or about King Josiah's reign in the years just after 627 B.C.E. seems to fit anything we can learn from the book of Jeremiah.

King Josiah's Reform

In particular, there is no word from Jeremiah about the reform of King Josiah in 622 B.C.E. This matter might well have been discussed above, but it is so important in itself that it requires special attention. This reform is described in detail in 2 Kings 22:3—23:24. Josiah sponsored a renovation of the Temple facilities, during which a scroll was discovered which purported to be the words of Moses to Israel. Scholars now believe that the description found in 2 Kings of that scroll best fits the book of Deuteronomy, or at least the core of the book of Deuteronomy (chaps. 5–26). It is altogether likely that the occasion of the discovery of the scroll was the time the book of Deuteronomy first came to public notice. Josiah, according to the account, was abashed at how far the public practice of religion had drifted from what the scroll enjoined. He consulted a prophetess, Huldah, who could certify the authenticity of the scroll, and he then had it read publicly and saw to it that the citizenry undertook to carry out its injunctions. He sponsored a total public reform on the basis of the various instructions of the scroll: all fertility cult worship was eliminated from the Temple area, and the priests in charge of fertility cults and astrological cults were turned out.

Further, all religious observances (i.e., sacrifices) outside of Jerusalem were forbidden, and the priests of those various centers were organized to take their turn in officiating at the sacrifices in Jerusalem (Deut. 18:6–8; 2 Kings 23:8); the festival of the Passover was reinstituted, according to the narrator, after a lapse of four hundred years (2 Kings 23:22); and there was in general an enormous bustle of public piety. One wonders, as a matter of fact, whether there was not political gain as well as religious virtue to be garnered from this reform: one recent authority suspects that the king's motive was at least partly to obtain an increase of tax receipts for Jerusalem.[4] But motives aside, reform did occur. No change in public religious practice as thoroughgoing had been made since Solomon's Temple was built.

What did Jeremiah say of this event? There is not a trace of reaction, positive or negative. Some scholars have tried to see in 8:9 a reference to Josiah's reform and Jeremiah's negative reaction to it; others have suggested that Jeremiah's appeal to adhere to "this covenant" in 11:1–13 is a reference to the reform and the prophet's positive reaction to it. However, neither of these passages specifically speaks of Josiah's reform, and I place each of them in other contexts later in Jeremiah's career (for 8:9, see chap. VI; for 11:1–13 see chap. IX). So, we find no word from Jeremiah on the reform.

The Foe from the North

There is no good candidate in this period for the "foe from the north" about whom Jeremiah often speaks. The Assyrians had stopped marching west; their successors, the Babylonians, had not yet begun marching—that would come later. Some decades ago scholars suggested that Jeremiah was speaking of the Scythians, a nomadic group from the far north (southern Russia) who, according to a rumor reported by the Greek historian Herodotus, invaded the Palestinian coast during those days. More recent studies, however, thoroughly discredit any Scythian invasion of Palestine,[5] and furthermore the description that Jeremiah gives of the foe from the north in no way fits the Scythians. Again, authorities have suggested that there is a mythological dimension to Jeremiah's descriptions of the foe.[6] My own view is that the foe is Babylon. I discuss this in chapter V.

A New Chronology

These difficulties in the traditional understanding of the chronology disappear if we assume that Jeremiah began to preach not in 627 B.C.E., but later—that the first time he came to real public notice was when he delivered his Temple Sermon at the beginning of the reign of King Jehoiakim in 609 B.C.E. (see chap. III). During Jehoiakim's reign there was evidently a reversion to some of the religious practices that King Josiah had outlawed (cf. 7:16–18).

Jeremiah was steadily at odds with Jehoiakim and his shortsighted ways. We have already noticed Jeremiah's contempt for him in 22:13–19 (see further the end of chap. III). The narrative of 36:11–32 gives a good picture of the king's attitude toward Jeremiah (see chap. VII). By 609 B.C.E. the reform of Josiah was history and no longer carefully enforced.

What, then, are we to make of the date 627 B.C.E., the thirteenth year of Josiah's reign, which we find in 1:2? Is it a mistake? No, I do not think so, and the clue is right in front of us, in 1:5.

> Before I formed you in the womb I knew you,
> and before you were born I consecrated you;
> I appointed you a prophet to the nations.

True, when he was a youth, Jeremiah responded to the call from Yahweh, but beyond that he sensed that Yahweh had *always* been knocking at the door of his life, even before he was born. I suggest, then, that 627 B.C.E., the thirteenth year of Josiah, is the date of Jeremiah's *birth*, and that whenever anyone would ask Jeremiah when the word of the Lord came to him, he would reply, with utter justification, "In the thirteenth year of Josiah," because "Before I formed you in the womb I knew you. . . ." If this assumption is correct, Jeremiah would have been five years old when Josiah instituted his great reform. Imagine the excited discussion the boy must have overheard in the household when his father Hilkiah learned that he must thereafter take his turn in going to Jerusalem to officiate at sacrifices—all because a scroll containing the words of Moses had just been read out in Jerusalem!

The Evidence of 15:16

There are two more pieces of evidence which suggest that Jeremiah cannot have begun to preach in 627 B.C.E. One I mention briefly—the meaning of the curious phrasing in 15:16, where Jeremiah is complaining to Yahweh that Yahweh has not looked after him properly (I discuss in chap. VIII the passage in which this verse appears). In the first line Jeremiah addresses Yahweh, "Your words were found, and I ate them." Some scholars simply assume that the phrase "your words were found" refers to the reception of the divine word by the prophet, but others are worried by the phrase, preferring to abandon the Hebrew wording altogether and follow the different text of the Greek Septuagint which connects v. 16 closely with the end of v. 15: "Know that for your sake I bear reproach from those who despise your words. Consume them, and your word will be the joy and delight of my heart."[7]

There is, however, no need to abandon the wording of the Hebrew text, which makes perfectly good sense. The only real parallel in the Old Testament for the expression "your words were found" is in the description of the finding of the scroll in the Temple in 2 Kings 22:13 and 23:2: "the words of the book (of the covenant) which had been found." I suggest, very simply, that the phrase "your words were found" in 15:16 is a poetic reference to the finding of the scroll in the Temple in 622 B.C.E., so that "and I ate them" refers to Jeremiah's own acceptance of Yahweh's call (similar to "Behold, I have put my words in your mouth," spoken by Yahweh to Jeremiah in 1:9). By this understanding of 15:16, Jeremiah must have accepted the call *after* the finding of the scroll in 622 B.C.E. and not before—and thus not in 627 B.C.E.

The other piece of evidence is the matter of Jeremiah's age at the time when he declares his celibacy (16:1–4); I shall deal with the question in chapter VII.

Jeremiah's Call

Now let us take a closer look at the words of the call itself as they are preserved in 1:4–10. Verse 5 says, "I appointed you a prophet to the nations." What would that mean?

First we need to get a clearer idea of what the Old Testament understands by the "word of Yahweh." The Hebrew expression *dābār*, usually translated in English as "word," also means "thing." This double meaning of *dābār* puzzles students until they begin to realize that for the Israelites "word" and "event" are part of the same perceived experience. What a person thinks and plans, what a person says, and what a person does, are all part of the *same* event. Spoken words, then, in the Israelite understanding, have the power to change situations fully as much as deeds do, and as powerfully; one has only to think of the deathbed "blessing" of Isaac in Genesis 27 or the "curses" reported elsewhere in the Old

Testament to realize how powerful words could be to the Israelites (e.g., Shimei's curse of King David in 2 Sam. 16:5–13, and the sequel in 1 Kings 2:8–9). Look up the law in Lev. 19:14! And of course when one speaks of *Yahweh's* word, it is a word that implies a deed as well, a deed at the time, or again a deed-to-be, a deed in the works. When we read, "And God said, 'Let there be light'" (Gen. 1:3), then there *was* light: just saying it does it. The best description of the power of Yahweh's word to get things done is found in Isa. 55:10–11. What is an "empty word"? An empty word is an echo, which returns without having accomplished anything. But Yahweh's word is not like that; it gets things done.

So for the prophet to speak Yahweh's word was an awesome thing. It was not just the equivalent of getting up and saying, "I suggest that the will of God for our day is thus and so." On the contrary, it was to let loose power for good or ill upon the people, as if someone were to smash a flask of deadly bacteria in a crowd— the bacteria are in the air; they are doing their work; and no one can call them back. The deed is done.

In Israel there was of course a long tradition of prophets, those who spoke for Yahweh. There was Nathan, who told King David he was wrong to steal Bathsheba from Uriah (2 Sam. 12:7); there was Elijah, who pronounced a drought (1 Kings 17:1) and told King Ahab he was wrong to steal the vineyard from Naboth (1 Kings 21:20); there were Amos and Hosea, Micah and Isaiah, and many more. Imagine what it would be like to feel in your bones that the end is coming upon your people (cf. Jer. 20:8–9). What if you felt that all is lost and that Yahweh has picked you out to do the telling to your people? What then? If you feel impelled to speak out that Jerusalem is destroyed (cf. 26:6, 9), then, though the walls and towers of Jerusalem be for the moment intact, their doom is sealed.

Toward the end of World War II the Germans used the castle of Colditz in the eastern part of the country as the prison for Allied officers who were recaptured after escaping from other German prisons. Colditz was reputed to be escape-proof and was reserved for the "bad boys." One day a British officer was seen planting minute amounts of dry rot into the beams of the castle. He argued that the RAF could remove the roof of a building in a second or so, but dry rot could do the same thing, though in a somewhat longer span of time—say, twenty years. Since the war might last that long, he was conceivably doing as much damage to the castle as a fair-sized bomb might.[8]

So with Jerusalem: the time would come when Jeremiah would be convinced that his very words would plant the dry rot in the timbers of Jerusalem. Look at 5:14: the word is fire, and burns! No wonder that when King Jehoiakim heard a scroll of Jeremiah's words being read he had the scroll burned (36:20–25). No wonder Jeremiah shrank from the task. (I look at 5:14 and the burning of the scroll in chap. VII.)

Notice, too, that Jeremiah's call is specifically to the "nations," plural, not simply to Judah alone. There are no limits to Yahweh's sovereignty, and so no limits to the scope of Jeremiah's ministry. No wonder that Jeremiah shrank from the task. He was too young, he believed.

The Prophet Like Moses

It is natural to wonder how Jeremiah perceived a call from Yahweh. While any answer is far past the reach of this inquiry, we may guess at some of the impulses that helped to prepare the way in which the prophet became aware of his call. In the case of Jeremiah, I have a suspicion about one factor, at least, that fed into his sense of Yahweh's pressing in upon his life, and that is a curious verse, Deut. 18:18:

> I will put my words in his mouth, and he shall speak to them all that I command him.

This verse, by my reconstruction, would have been a part of the scroll found in the Temple when Jeremiah was five years old. The verse states that Yahweh told Moses that someday, long after Moses, Yahweh would raise up another prophet, a prophet like Moses, who would continue the process of announcing Yahweh's word to the people. The wording by which Jeremiah perceived Yahweh's call—"Behold, I have put my words in your mouth" (1:9), and "whatever I command you you shall speak" (1:7)—is very close to the wording of Deut. 18:18 that speaks of the prophet like Moses. No other call of a prophet in the Old Testament resembles this verse in Deuteronomy as closely. There may be other possible explanations for the similarity of wording, but I think it is easiest to understand it as Jeremiah's conviction that *he* is the prophet like Moses.

From the task of being a prophet he shrank. But Moses, too, had hesitated in accepting his own call: the narrative in Exod. 4:1–17 is vivid with Moses' objections to Yahweh regarding the task that Yahweh was laying on him. Jeremiah, then, was like Moses *even in his hesitation*. Jeremiah felt boxed in. Moses' excuse to Yahweh was that he was an incompetent public speaker (Exod. 4:10); Jeremiah's, that he was too young (1:6).

An Opportunity for Jeremiah to Hear Deuteronomy?

In Deut. 31:10–13 we read of the provision made to recite the law of Deuteronomy: it is to be read publicly every seven years, at the time of the "feast of booths." The feast of booths, or tabernacles, is the great autumnal festival at the end of September or beginning of October; in our day it culminates with Yom Kippur, the Day of Atonement. If Deuteronomy was first proclaimed publicly in 622 B.C.E. during Josiah's reforms, then at seven-year intervals it would be proclaimed again in 615 B.C.E. and 608 B.C.E. But as we shall see in chapter III, by 608 B.C.E. Jeremiah was already in the public eye; his Temple Sermon is to be dated to the fall of 609 B.C.E. One wonders, however, about the reading of Deuteronomy in 615 B.C.E. Jeremiah, by my calculation, would have been twelve years old. Was he part of the assembly of all Israel—men, women, and little ones (Deut. 31:12)—gathered in Jerusalem to hear the reading of the law? Is this when he was struck by hearing the words about the prophet like Moses to come? Is this when he was overwhelmed by the sense of his destiny to be like Moses, to speak for Yahweh to his generation? Our first reaction to the idea is to push it aside: surely twelve is far too young an age to be grasped by such an idea. But Luke records the tradition that Jesus, at the age of twelve, was asking questions of the teachers in the temple and amazing witnesses with his understanding (Luke 2:42, 46–47). Of course with regard to Jeremiah there is no certainty in such speculation. In any event, whether he was twelve or a few years older when he accepted his call, it is clear that he himself protests to Yahweh that he is too young.

The Required Assurance
from Yahweh

It is important to understand the Israelite attitude toward the young. It was probably a good deal like the attitude of the peoples in the Middle East today toward their young people. In the traditional cultures of Turkey, the Arab world, Iran, it is the elders who have wisdom, who give orders and advice, who are looked up to. Young people defer to their elders and wait their turn, that is, until they are of suitable age themselves. Even the children sort themselves out by age: younger brothers defer to the eldest brother, who is always the boss. In our own culture, by contrast, there is a great deal of cultivation of youth and a great deal of envy on the part of older people for the vitality of young people.

But in Old Testament times young people deferred to the elders, and Jeremiah must have felt the disability of his youth keenly. Who would ever listen to him as he spoke out to his fellow citizens in the name of the Lord God Almighty and modeled his words after those of Moses of old?

The words that Jeremiah would be impelled to speak out would not be welcome. And Jeremiah for his part could sense that there would be nothing but opposition ahead. This suspicion was based not only on what he himself could calculate in the way of risks but more specifically, I think, on the worrisome words of Psalm 22, a psalm that was undoubtedly known to him.

The first eleven verses of the psalm are the lament of an Israelite who feels himself abandoned by God and hedged in by mocking foes. We are so accustomed to reading this psalm as a description of Jesus, who spoke out the opening phrase while hanging on the cross (Mark 15:34), that we forget for how many years that psalm had fed the souls of earlier Israelites. I suggest, however, not that Jeremiah would have been alarmed in general by words that speak of abandonment by God, but that this psalm would have seemed to Jeremiah a specific description of *Moses'* own experience. In Exod. 1:22 Pharaoh orders every male child to be "cast" into the Nile; in Psalm 22:10 the psalmist says, "Upon you [God] was I cast from my birth" (the same Hebrew verb, *hashlīk*, is used in both passages). Indeed, the description in vv. 9–10 fits the story of Moses' birth and infancy closely. Jeremiah surely had heard these words as Moses' story and wondered whether accepting the task of being the prophet like Moses would not also include persecution after the fashion of Psalm 22.

Hence the necessity for Jeremiah, in 1:8, to hear reassurance from Yahweh that Yahweh would look after him. It may be sound theology to say, as people do sometimes, that "one person with God is a majority," but it is still a frightening thing to be that one person against the multitude; one had better be sure that God is available for help after all. What we have, then, is a kind of deal: If I, Jeremiah, am to speak for you, Yahweh, to your people, then you, Yahweh, are to look after me. This is the assumption upon which Jeremiah depends as he is launched into his career, and this assumption is at the root of the extraordinary complaints that he will lodge with Yahweh, complaints I examine in chapters VIII and IX.

The call is an awesome one; we have said that. But look at the wording of Jer. 1:10. It is a verse of tightknit poetry; its structure can be seen if we omit the middle two verbs ("to destroy and to overthrow"), which are the addition of a later editor. We then have:

> See, I have set you this day over nations and over kingdoms,
> to pluck up and to break down,
> to build and to plant.

The scope of Jeremiah's responsibility is international, and his task is both destructive and constructive. But destruction first, alas. Notice the nice X-form of the four verbs of his task: to uproot and to smash, to build and to plant—two of the verbs have to do with trees, and the other two with houses. They are arranged, as I say, in an X-form (i.e., "chiasmus," so called because the Greek letter chi is in the form of an X). And the verbs almost rhyme, too:

> *lintōsh welintōṣ*
> *libnōt welintō'*

We will recognize and appreciate Jeremiah's poetic skill at many points in this study.

Jeremiah's Call Symbolized

To the account of the call that we have been examining are appended two "visions" in vv. 11–14. Inasmuch as these visionary experiences are placed just after Jeremiah's call, it is altogether likely that they came early in the prophet's career.

The first concerns a sprig of flowering almond. Jeremiah was out walking one day and had a glimpse of the flowering almond; this reassured him that Yahweh really would back up his word through Jeremiah to the people. What is involved here? The almond blossom has the Hebrew name of "watcher" *(shāqēd)* presumably because in its early blooming it "watches" *(shōqēd)* for the spring. Some years ago, when I was teaching in Beirut, Lebanon, a group of us were visiting the Jerusalem area. One morning during that visit our bus took us north of Jerusalem to the site of the biblical city of Gibeon, a spot that is just a few miles west of Jeremiah's Anathoth. It was a foggy morning early in February, and in the village where the ruins of the city are to be found we glimpsed, through the white fog, a whole orchard of almond trees in full white blossom. It was a sight I shall never forget, and I have wondered since then whether it was not on such a morning that Jeremiah caught his glimpse of the almond tree in bloom.

To Jeremiah the almond carried a message, and the message was wrapped up in the name of the blossom: as Jeremiah had seen the almond blossom *(shāqēd)*, so Yahweh would be watching *(shōqēd)* over his word, to bring it to pass. It is easy to imagine Jeremiah both brooding over the whole issue of Yahweh's message to his people and wondering whether Yahweh would make the word come to pass that the prophet felt impelled to speak. Does this word, too, have power? And brooding, brooding over this one terrible question, Jeremiah found his attention caught by a glimpse of the almond. The glimpse came as an answer to his question, and the answer was in the form of a pun or wordplay.

To us a pun is usually a bad joke and little more; it is hard for us to imagine how a mere word association might represent serious thought, let alone a message from God. But, in those days, the Israelites used word associations with the name of someone who had died to create a dirge to mark that person's death, and nothing would seem more serious than a funeral lament. Thus the death of

Abner (in Hebrew, '*abnēr*) suggested the word "fool" (in Hebrew, *nābāl*), so that David began his lament for Abner with the words, "Should Abner die as a fool dies?" (2 Sam. 3:33). Words, as we have seen, had power for the Israelites; and the power resided not only in their *meanings*, that gave rise to action, but in their *sounds* as well. Words then became a channel for unexpected communication. To you and me, word association does not seem a very secure basis for faith in God, but it did seem secure enough to Jeremiah, and it is he whom we are trying to understand. And then again, there have been many other channels by which people through the centuries have understood themselves to receive word or strength from God—dreams, for example—that seem insubstantial to the doubter but substantial to the believer.

Jeremiah's second vision is concerned not with the power behind the word from Yahweh but with the message, the content, of that word. Unfortunately both what he sees and what it means are difficult to discern. The end of v. 13 reads, "I see a pot being fanned, whose rim is away from the north" (my trans.). Most commentators believe that the pot is full of water and that it is about to overflow from the north, but as far as I can see the text implies nothing about water boiling over or spilling. In Ezek. 24:11 we read of an empty cooking-pot being heated on hot coals, being charred so that the pot can be cleaned of the baked-on food remains. I propose that Jeremiah saw something similar, a cooking-pot lying on its side, being cleaned of the remains of food.

I suspect that Jeremiah had two different interpretations of this vision, each at a different time, one when he experienced it and another one some years later. He first understood this vision to signify Yahweh's intention to subject the tribes of the north (the people of the northern kingdom of Israel, exiled by Assyria a hundred years before) to judgment and purification (v. 16). Then, some years later, he understood the vision to signify Yahweh's bringing the foe from the north, Babylon, down upon Jerusalem (v. 15). But the question is an intricate one, and so is the question of the function of vv. 17–19, words that I believe Jeremiah heard still later in his career, perhaps in 594 B.C.E. (the matter is mentioned again in chap. IX). Struggling with these questions would take us too far afield; we had best stop at this point.

And, indeed, we have come a long way in this chapter. We have tried to see the turmoil in the mind of the young Jeremiah as he sensed that Yahweh was calling him to be the prophet like Moses, a task he fought against accepting. He did accept it, reluctantly, strengthened by the conviction that Yahweh would back up his word and back up the prophet who spoke that word.

And so the young man went out to preach. What he preached we must now consider.

NOTES

1. For an old tradition about the Ark of the Covenant in Moses' day, see Num. 10:35–36.

2. The evidence is a bit uncertain but is perhaps to be pieced together from the data in 1 Sam. 2:27–36; 14:3; 22:18–23; and 2 Sam. 8:17. The whole matter is discussed briefly in R. W. Corney, "Abiathar," in *The Interpreter's Dictionary of the Bible* (Nashville: Abingdon Press, 1962), I: 6–7; and idem, "Eli," in *Interpreter's Dictionary of the Bible*, II:85. Cf. John Bright, *Jeremiah*, Anchor Bible (Garden City, N.Y.: Doubleday & Co., 1965), lxxxvii–lxxxviii.

3. The only scholar who has written for the general public who disagrees with the traditional chronology, and who comes to a solution similar to the one I propose here, is J. Philip Hyatt; see his introduction and exegesis on Jeremiah in *The Interpreter's Bible* (New York: Abingdon Press, 1956), V:779–80, 797–98. For others who take this view, see my *Jeremiah 2*, Hermeneia (Minneapolis: Augsburg Fortress, 1989), 25 nn. 125, 126, 127.

4. For a study of this matter, see Stanley B. Frost, "The Death of Josiah, A Conspiracy of Silence," *Journal of Biblical Literature* 87 (1968): 369–82.

5. See Richard P. Vaggione, "All Over Asia? The Extent of the Scythian Domination in Herodotus," *Journal of Biblical Literature* 92 (1973): 523–30.

6. Brevard S. Childs, *Myth and Reality in the Old Testament* (Naperville, Ill.: Alec R. Allenson, 1960), 87.

7. For the assumption that the phrase "your words were found" refers to the reception of the divine word by the prophet, see the German commentary by Artur Weiser, *Das Buch Jeremia* (Göttingen: Vandenhoeck & Ruprecht, 1969), 133. Among those who express uneasiness at the phrase is the German scholar F. Giesebrecht in *Das Buch Jeremia* (Göttingen: Vandenhoeck & Ruprecht, 1907), 92, who calls it "a somewhat drastic expression." J. Philip Hyatt follows the Greek text: see his commentary in

the *Interpreter's Bible*, V:942, where he cites earlier commentators who choose the same solution.

8. P. R. Reid, *The Colditz Story* (London: Hodder & Stoughton, 1952), chap. XVII.

A SERMON AT THE TEMPLE

After 627 B.C.E., the next recorded event in Jeremiah's life for which we have a date is a sermon he delivered in the Temple area in the fall of 609 B.C.E. This sermon was so memorable that there is notice of it in two passages in the book of Jeremiah—chapters 7 and 26. Jeremiah 7:1–15 simply gives the wording of the sermon. (I believe the original sermon includes only vv. 1–12; vv. 13–15, I believe, are an addition by Jeremiah some years later when it became clear that the people were not responding to his words.) Chapter 26, by contrast, is narrative; it summarizes the sermon in vv. 1–4 and 6 (I think v. 5 is an addition from later times) and then in vv. 7–24 tells what happened immediately after Jeremiah preached it. Both passages obviously reflect the same event: notice, for example, the mention of "Shiloh" in both 7:12 and 26:6 (cf. 26:9).

The date of the fall of 609 B.C.E. is gained from 26:1: "In the beginning of the reign of Jehoiakim the son of Josiah, king of Judah." It had been a stunning half-year, with three kings successively on the throne in Jerusalem. To appreciate this we must go back a bit and pick up a little more history.

As I noted, Nineveh, the capital of Assyria, in northern Mesopotamia, fell to the Babylonian army in 612 B.C.E. The refugee Assyrian government moved 240 miles west to Haran, a city near the Balikh River, a tributary of the Euphrates (its location is about midway along the present northern border of Syria, and just north of that border in southern Turkey). Two years later, in 610 B.C.E., the Babylonian army drove the Assyrians from Haran as well. At this point a new Pharaoh, Neco II, ascended the throne of Egypt. He decided that the Babylonian presence at Haran was too close for comfort, so the following spring (609 B.C.E.) the Egyptian army marched north to try to help the Assyrians regain Haran. (It might seem cynical of the Egyptians to try to *help* their old enemy Assyria, but government policy is often shaped by the notion that "the enemy of my enemy is my friend.")

King Josiah of Judah had no liking for the march of an Egyptian army through his realm, particularly when that Egyptian army was coming to the rescue of Assyria, Judah's old enemy. He therefore attempted to block the progress of the Egyptian army at Megiddo (about fifty-five miles north of Jerusalem), but in so doing he fell in battle. This entire episode is summarized in a single verse in the Bible (2 Kings 23:29). The news must have stunned Judah: here was a king who, according to the narrator, was unparalleled in goodness (see 2 Kings 23:25), struck down at the age of only thirty-nine; 2 Chron. 35:25 records that his death was commemorated for generations.

Then, according to 2 Kings 23:30, Jehoahaz, a younger son of Josiah, was placed on the throne by "the people of the land," probably the country gentry who hoped Jehoahaz would continue the policies of his father.

In the meantime the Egyptian Pharaoh had not succeeded in driving the Babylonians from Haran, so he turned back, established a power base at Carchemish on the upper Euphrates (fifty-five miles west of Haran), and thereby consolidated his power in Syria and Palestine. He summoned the young King Jehoahaz of Judah, who had been on the throne only three months, to his headquarters at Riblah (sixty-five miles north of Damascus), deposed and arrested him, and put the older brother of Jehoahaz, Jehoiakim, on the throne, taking Jehoahaz captive back to Egypt, where he died (2 Kings 23:31–34). Jehoahaz would have come to the throne roughly in June of 609 B.C.E., and Jehoiakim would have been put on the throne approximately in September of that year.[1]

Jeremiah offered a short poem on the situation at that time (22:10). He urged people to mourn not for Josiah but rather for Jehoahaz, who has gone away never to return. Jeremiah 22:11–12 is then a prose commentary on the poem; as 1 Chron. 3:15 indicates, "Shallum" was another name for Jehoahaz.

Jehoiakim may have been the older son of Josiah, but he seems to have shown no interest in continuing the religious reform begun by his father, as Jeremiah must surely have been aware. The death of Josiah, the three-month reign of Jehoahaz, and the advent of a man such as Jehoiakim must have impelled Jeremiah to speak out at the Temple.

As we have seen, 26:1 gives the date of the sermon as "the beginning of the reign of Jehoiakim." Here the word "beginning" seems to be a technical term for the fraction of a year a new king reigns before the first New Year's Day, at which point the "first" year of the king's reign is reckoned. The new year evidently began in the spring (March or April), so the "beginning" of Jehoiakim's reign would have begun the previous fall, the fall of 609 B.C.E. A likely occasion would have been the festival of booths (tabernacles), the "high holy days" at the end of September or the beginning of October, when Jeremiah would have addressed the crowds coming to worship (7:2; 26:2).

The Sermon:
Jeremiah 7:1–12; 26:7–24

I begin by calling attention to what seems to be a play on words on Jeremiah's part, whose meaning was lost on later generations. In the RSV, both 7:3 and 7:7 have "I will let you dwell in this place." However, in the NRSV the translation in v. 3 is, "Let me dwell with you in this place," and similarly in v. 7 the translation is, "I will dwell with you in this place." Which is correct? The Hebrew text of the Old Testament was originally written *with consonants alone*; the vowels had to be supplied by the readers in the course of the reading. The traditional Hebrew reading that has come down to us in both verses is, "I will let you dwell," but the ancient Latin translation made by St. Jerome in the fourth century C.E. (the Vulgate) puts a different set of vowels to the consonantal text and reads, "I will dwell with you."

If we look at the way the sermon proceeds, v. 3 is about the Temple (cf. v. 4), while v. 7 is about the "land which I gave of old to your fathers for ever." I therefore propose that in v. 3 we must read, with St. Jerome, "I will dwell with you in this place" (the Temple); here, then, the NRSV would be correct. In v. 7, though, we must read, with the traditional Hebrew reading, "I will let you dwell in this place" (i.e., the land of Palestine); here we must follow the RSV. Jeremiah was evidently engaging in wordplay here, using the same consonants for two different phrases. But since the written Hebrew text of the phrases of both v. 3 and v. 7 in Jeremiah's day simply offered the same set of consonants without contrasting vowels, it proved impossible for the tradition to hold on to the wordplay.

Make Your Ways and Doings Good:
Jeremiah 7:1–12

The sermon begins with the command, "Amend your ways and your doings." This literally reads, "Make your ways and your doings good," with the implication that this would be better than "evil doings" (26:3). If the people do make their ways and their doings good rather than evil, then Yahweh will continue to make a dwelling place with them *in the Temple:* people should not simply trust in the formula "This is the Temple of the Lord, the Temple of the Lord, the Temple of the Lord." Why does Jeremiah say it three times? Is he mocking the tendency of those in Jerusalem to substitute a slogan for reality?

How plausible was it for people to cling to the notion that the Temple in Jerusalem was the ultimate sanctuary from disaster? Recall that when the Assyrian army had besieged Jerusalem in 701 B.C.E., the prophet Isaiah had reassured the people that Jerusalem would not fall; Isaiah's reassurance must have encouraged the belief that Jerusalem was invulnerable. Then in 622 B.C.E. King Josiah centralized the worship of Yahweh in the Jerusalem Temple: this move, too, must have reinforced the conviction of the permanent place of the Temple in Yahweh's plan. People must have felt, "We have done our part for Yahweh, so now Yahweh will do Yahweh's part for us."

The slogan, "This is the Temple of the Lord," may not only reflect the people's trust in the invulnerability of the Temple, but also betray their urge to cover over their deep unease. This may parallel what happened in the summer of 1940, soon after the beginning of World War II. Paris fell to the German armies, something that had not happened even in the worst days of the Franco-Prussian War or World War I. And then the Battle of Britain began in the air. At that point we in the United States began to see stickers in the windows of cars reading, "There will always be an England," a slogan that conveyed both faith and fear. So perhaps in Jerusalem in 609 B.C.E. the sentiment was similar: Egypt was supreme; what will happen next? "There will always be a Temple." "This is the Temple of the Lord."

So also with regard to the land. If the people make their ways and doings good, Yahweh will allow them to live in the land which was a divine gift given to their ancestors (v. 7). The land was given to the people, yes, but that does not mean, given the gift, that they can play fast and loose and persist in "evil doings" (26:3). In 7:6 Jeremiah spells out in detail what "make your ways and your doings good" will mean, in expressions that in Hebrew emphasize the positive: literally, "If you really do make your ways and your doings good—if each of you really does do justice between yourself and your neighbor, if you do not oppress the stranger, the orphan, and the widow, and if you do not walk after other gods to your own hurt—then I will let you live in this place" (my trans.). Doing good involves three instances of good behavior: (1) justice between equals; (2) care for the helpless in the community; and (3) faithfulness to Yahweh rather than to competing gods. These three actions scarcely need to be explained; they typify what Yahweh requires of the covenant people. I shall be discussing them, especially the matter of the temptation to worship the competing fertility god Baal, throughout this book (see chap. IV).

If the people continue to make their ways and their doings good, then Yahweh will let them continue to dwell in the land; if not, Yahweh will not. In that case, as the summary in 26:6 reads, Yahweh will make "this city" a curse for all the nations of the earth.

Verse 8 again warns the people against trusting deceptive words, doubtless words such as the slogan in v. 4. But if v. 4 was a prohibition against such trust, v. 8 is an accusation that the people have been doing just that and, moreover, that they also have been breaking the Ten Commandments and then blithely coming into the Temple with the words "We are delivered!" on their lips and without any thought of the contradiction between their words and actions (vv. 9–10). Is it cynicism on the part of the people or some kind of terrible insensitivity that they do not see the contradiction?

Verse 11 is hard to render in smooth English, but it sounds something like this: "Is a robbers' cave what my house which is called by my name has become in your eyes? Very well: I have kept my eyes open too!" Jeremiah here understands Yahweh to be describing the Temple as the headquarters of thugs. This language must have been even more shocking when Jeremiah used it than it was when Jesus repeated it in the Temple area in his day (Mark 11:17). "In your eyes" means both "in your sight" and "in your judgment"; that is, you do know better, but you have deliberately distorted the purpose of the Temple. To this Yahweh adds, All right, but I have eyes too.

In a last twist of the knife Yahweh suggests, "If you have eyes, go north to the place of my sanctuary at Shiloh and see what I did to it in the face of the evil of my people Israel" (v. 12). By mentioning Shiloh, Yahweh challenges the people by using the only kind of argument that had any chance of being understood: historical experience. But the people may have conspired to keep silence about what had happened at Shiloh. Remember that Shiloh had been the central sanctuary of the Israelites in the early days, the place where Samuel grew up; and we have seen how the village of Anathoth may have preserved its old traditions (chap. II). After Samuel reached adulthood, the enemy Philistines from the west captured Shiloh, took away the sacred Ark of the Covenant, which had symbolized God's presence with the Israelite army, and then evidently destroyed the sanctuary there (cf. 1 Samuel 4). The Israelites eventually regained possession of the Ark of the Covenant—the Philistines were superstitiously fearful of its power (1 Sam. 5:6–12)—but Shiloh never again became a sanctuary for the Israelites. There is no account in 1 Samuel of the burning of Shiloh (was the event too painful to be remembered?), and there is only one other passage in the Old Testament that even indirectly indicates what had happened: we read in Psalm 78:60, "He [Yahweh] forsook his dwelling at Shiloh, the tent where he dwelt among men."

Jeremiah's message is plain: there was no *need* on Yahweh's part for the Temple at Jerusalem, any more than there had been a need for the sanctuary at Shiloh. Yahweh uses the Jerusalem Temple so long as the worshipers there really adhere to covenant norms, but Yahweh does not need the structure. Indeed, Yahweh is as capable of burning down the Temple in Jerusalem as of burning down the former sanctuary at Shiloh. But, people would certainly wonder, what about the "gospel according to Isaiah," the good news that Jerusalem is inviolable? The answer that Jeremiah would give is that Yahweh is not bound by an earlier decision: *Yahweh can revoke it.* Just as the decision in Isaiah's day was to save Jerusalem, now Yahweh can decide to destroy Jerusalem. But that decision will not be carried out if Israel changes its ways (26:3, 13)! This sense of an unconstrained God, a God not bound by any habits or past behavior, must have been appalling to those worshiping in Jerusalem, especially to the religious establishment of Jerusalem, bound as it was by a careful adherence to the habits and procedures of the past.

With the vision of an unconstrained God comes the corollary: cultic observances, the proper sacrifices, are not *sufficient* to please Yahweh. They may be necessary, part of the given of Yahweh's expectations, but they are never sufficient. In this Jeremiah was only echoing what earlier prophets had pronounced (cf. Amos 5:21–24 and Isa. 1:12–17 among many such passages). Worship unaccompanied by deeds is empty (7:10). It is easy to make this affirmation, but it is hard to remember it.

Official Reaction to the Sermon:
Jeremiah 26:7–24

It is of course the religious authorities who first hear Jeremiah ("the priests and the prophets," 26:7). What do they object to? According to v. 9, what catches their attention is Jeremiah's reference to the possible destruction of both the Temple and the city. According to the record, they call the civil authorities over from the palace nearby ("the princes," vv. 10 and 11) and report Jeremiah's speech to them. Is their summary in v. 11 only a casual abbreviation of the sermon? Or is it significant that when they repeat Jeremiah's offending words, they omit his reference to the Temple and speak only of Jeremiah's prophesying against the city (v. 11)? To the princes this would make the issue appear to be treason rather than a religious dispute.

The civil authorities then hold a trial (vv. 10–16), the fullest description we have in the Old Testament of Israelite trial procedure. Jeremiah's defense in vv. 12–15 is simple: Do as you wish with me. But you must understand that I do not speak for myself; I am a spokesman for Yahweh—it is Yahweh who has sent me. So if you kill me, you will be calling Yahweh's anger down upon yourselves and upon the city for which you are responsible.

This statement has the effect of arousing the religious fears of the princes, and they find the civil complaint of the religious leadership without basis. The princes accordingly turn the matter back to the religious authorities, saying, in effect, This does not concern us, it is your responsibility. After all, the man speaks for Yahweh (v. 16).

An elder breaks the impasse: as Jeremiah had cited Shiloh as a precedent, so the elder cites a precedent for this situation. The prophet Micah, over a hundred years before, he points out, prophesied the destruction of both the Temple area and the city in a similar fashion (vv. 17–18; see Micah 3:12), and King Hezekiah did not put *him* to death. This precedent is enough to save Jeremiah's life.

Nonetheless, the king could not have been pleased by Jeremiah's sermon, and the narrative adds an account, in vv. 20–23, of another prophet whose message was similar to Jeremiah's, the prophet Uriah. The king tried to kill Uriah, but Uriah escaped to Egypt. The king, however, sent a posse led by a man named Elnathan son of Achbor to Egypt (recall that Egypt was the sponsor of the king). He arrested Uriah and brought him back to the king, who executed him and threw his body in the community burying ground. Let Jeremiah be warned! It was fortunate that a courtier named Ahikam son of Shaphan was friendly to Jeremiah and protected him (v. 24).

Prophecy as Blasphemy or Treason

Jeremiah walked the way countless others since his time have walked: one thinks of Socrates and Jesus and so many others, who have been called subversive and threatened with death, who have been sentenced to death and had the sentence carried out, all because they dared to question what people have taken to be true.

Those who live decades and centuries later may see clearly how the words of a fresh thinker have been vindicated by subsequent events, but such second-guessing does not necessarily lead to greater wisdom when another fresh thinker comes along.

It was peculiarly difficult for Jeremiah's peers to understand how Yahweh might level a judgmental word against the religious establishment, for of course the whole experience of monarchy in Israel and Judah had reinforced the identification between church and state. Once a nationalistic enterprise is deemed to be sacred, once a nation-state is understood to be the expression of the will of God, it is peculiarly difficult for people to accept any challenge to the system. Jeremiah was forced to take account of the issue, in his day, as to whether "church" needed to be "state" as well, and whether either could be identified with the will of God. Public reaction was quick and stiff. Jeremiah was threatened with death, and not for the last time (see chaps. VII and XI).

Jeremiah 22:13–19. Of course King Jehoiakim could not have reacted favorably to Jeremiah's sermon. It is also clear that Jeremiah had no respect for the king. In chapter II we noted Jeremiah's positive assessment of King Josiah in comparison to his negative assessment of Jehoiakim (22:13–19). Since that oracle probably was uttered early in Jehoiakim's reign, it is appropriate to examine it at this time.

During the first years of his reign, according to 2 Kings 23:35, Jehoiakim had to tax "the people of the land" (as noted earlier, perhaps the rural gentry) in order to raise the tribute money he was obligated to send to Egypt. This taxation must have aroused widespread resentment in places like Anathoth, Jeremiah's town. Furthermore the king evidently embarked upon a fresh building project, either building a new palace or renovating the old one, and to this end he drafted the citizens of Judah for work-parties (22:13–14). Jeremiah's word from Yahweh on this matter is scathing: Imagine trying to be king by competing in cedar! (22:15). The verse continues by noting that a king can act with justice and righteousness and still be a king: Jehoiakim's father Josiah had. The phrase occurring in both vv. 15 and 16, "Then it was well (with him)," means either (1) "he still managed to eat and drink and live well," or (2) "things went well for him as head of the covenant people," or (3) both of these.

But, the oracle continues in v. 17, the king can think only of his "dishonest gain" (lit. his "cut") and of shedding the blood of the innocent, extortion, and committing oppression—precisely what the worshipers in the Temple were warned not to do (7:6, 9). As a result, the oracle concludes, when the king dies he will receive none of the expected mourning rites, and indeed will be given the burial of an ass, his corpse simply dragged outside the city gates. The king's glory, built up so insubstantially, will merit nothing but degradation when he dies. In David's lament over Abner the king asks rhetorically, "Should Abner die as a fool dies?" (2 Sam. 3:33: see p. 22), the implied answer being, "Of course not." But Jeremiah affirms most positively that Jehoiakim will die as an ass dies.

Jeremiah 17:11. There is one more passage that I believe might fit chronologically here, and that is a single verse in Jeremiah that stands by itself: 17:11. I translate the verse as,

> Like the partridge that broods but does not hatch is he who makes riches, but not with justice: midway in his days he will abandon them, and at his end he will be a fool.

This verse sounds like a proverb, something akin to, "Don't count your chickens before they're hatched," and indeed in a way it is. But it is likely that Jeremiah directed it specifically to King Jehoiakim: the phrase "but not with justice" is very close in Hebrew to "by injustice" in 22:13. The poor foolish partridge lays her eggs all over the place and is never sure of hatching them all. It is humiliating then to be compared to a poor bird that cannot protect its eggs, the more so if one happens to be king.

The time will come when Jeremiah will have a full-scale confrontation with King Jehoiakim (see chap. VII). For now we simply ponder the situation of a prophet who is on a collision course with the reigning monarch and who prophesies what sounds to the king like sedition or treason.

NOTES

1. The problems of reconstructing the chronology are difficult. I follow here the reconstruction of John Gray, *I and II Kings* (Philadelphia: Westmin-

ster Press, 1970), 749; and Abraham Malamat, "The Twilight of Judah," in *Congress Volume, Edinburgh, 1974*, Supplements to Vetus Testamentum 28 (Leiden: E. J. Brill, 1975), 124–27. A different view is given in John H. Hayes and Paul K. Hooker, *A New Chronology for the Kings of Israel and Judah and Its Implications for Biblical History and Literature* (Atlanta: John Knox Press, 1988), 88–90.

IV | GOD'S PEOPLE TURN THEIR BACKS

Chapter 2 of the book of Jeremiah begins a collection of Jeremiah's oracles, short utterances in poetic form that were understood by him to be words from Yahweh to the people; this particular collection extends through 4:4.

The Faithful Israel: Jeremiah 2:1–3

Jeremiah 2 opens with a short poem that stands by itself, a picture of the loyalty and faithfulness to Yahweh that Israel had maintained in the early days of their relationship.

> I remember the devotion of your youth,
>   your love as a bride,
> how you followed me in the wilderness,
>   in a land not sown.
> Israel was holy to the Lord,
>   the first fruits of his harvest.
> All who ate of it were held guilty;
>   disaster came upon them,
>   says the Lord.
>
> (2:2–3, NRSV)

Here, at the very beginning, we see many of the characteristics of Old Testament poetry, and of Jeremiah's poetry in particular. We see the typical parallelism, in which a second line renews or reinforces the first line by using a synonymous or supplementing image. We see the concentration of images and ideas, so that we are forced to listen to them slowly and explore their implications. Let us try it.

Remember. Israelite remembering is not idle recollection. I might say, "I can't really remember what my grandfather looked like, he died so many years ago," and such a remark may be of only casual interest. But to the Israelite way of thinking, remembering is the way by which the past is recaptured in power for the present moment, almost as if there is a residue of energy in the past that can be appropriated and can make a real difference to the present situation. Thus for Yahweh to say, "I remember" the devotion of Israel in the past suggests, so to speak, that Yahweh is taking the file marked "Israel" and moving it from the inactive to the active basket. Yahweh is going to *do* something about Israel's situation. "I am taking account of" or "I am taking notice of" are clumsy paraphrases, but they will have to do. (This biblical view of memory has great consequence for the New Testament as well. When Jesus says, "Do this in remembrance of me," he is not urging us to hold a memorial service but rather to allow God to reenact the old event in all its present power.)

Devotion. This important word (Heb. *ḥesed*) is often translated "steadfast love" in the RSV and NRSV (e.g., in the refrain lines of Psalm 136). It means the loyalty that two partners have for each other even when circumstances are no longer so happy. Husband and wife in a sturdy marriage stick by each other even when many kinds of disaster pile upon them at once. This is *ḥesed*. "I am now taking account of the dogged fidelity you once showed me in your honeymoon days" is what is indicated here.

In the wilderness. This suggests "when disaster threatened," that no one is comfortable in a wilderness, where food and drink and security are at a minimum.

Holy. This word had little of the stained-glass tone for Jeremiah that it has for us. Deep down, it had to do with those people, things, or characteristics that belong to God, with what God owns or has charge of. "Israel belonged to Yahweh" is really what the phrase means here; Israel was special to Yahweh, Israel was set aside for Yahweh's purposes. Nothing is said directly about Israel being morally pure, though that would be indirectly involved. An apt parallel is the chalice many churches keep on their altars, reserved for use in the service of communion. We would not think it appropriate to walk up to the altar on a hot day and use the chalice to have a drink of iced tea; it is simply not done. The chalice is special; it belongs to communion. Israel was special to Yahweh in just that way.

The first fruits of his harvest. This phrase continues the meaning of "holy" as "belonging to Yahweh." Traditionally, whatever was first in the agricultural year belonged to Yahweh—the first lamb of the flock (Exod. 13:11–16), the first sheaf of wheat (Deut. 26:1–4). There were ceremonies established for offering the first fruits to Yahweh (Deut. 26:5–10). Here in 2:3, as later passages will indicate (2:21; 5:10–11), Jeremiah evidently has the grape harvest in mind: Israel has been as special to Yahweh as the first fruits of the vintage are. (The prophet Isaiah, a hundred years earlier, had offered the same idea: in Isa. 5:1–7 the prophet set forth a parable of Israel as the vineyard of Yahweh.)

All who ate of it were held guilty. Jeremiah continues the image in this line. Any tribe or nation that tried to gain victory over Israel got into trouble for doing so. The last verb, *'āsham,* means more than "became guilty" (RSV); it means "took upon themselves the consequences of their wrongdoing." It is not just that those enemy peoples *found* themselves in the wrong; they *paid* for their wrongdoing as well, by suffering failure and defeat. Indeed the balancing line that follows says it: *"Disaster came upon them."* Militarily and socially, Israel was a success in those early days because the nation had remained utterly faithful to Yahweh. We might go on to say that Israel's wars against other nations in those early days were holy wars, with Yahweh leading the army, strange though the idea may seem to us. So, at least, Jeremiah reads the past.

We may register astonishment today at the freedom with which the prophets presumed to explain the past in terms of their own present situation. Perhaps to some degree this is something we all do, but certainly the prophets did not feel any necessity to toe a party line in their interpretation of history. So 2:2–3 stands in contrast to Ezek. 20:13, in which the prophet Ezekiel was moved to say that Israel had *never* been faithful to Yahweh, even in the wilderness period; Israel, it seems, had always been rebellious. Perhaps each prophet found raw material in the nation's memories to serve as example for his own reconstruction of the past.

Here, in any event, is Jeremiah's picture of the pristine purity of

Israel: Israel had been faithful, and therefore successful, in the past.

The Unfaithful Israel

Jeremiah 2:5–13

How great is the contrast with the present situation! This Jeremiah sets forth in a series of poems beginning with 2:5. These poems, as we have them, are not necessarily in chronological order; instead, one senses here a kind of artistic order, the poem in vv. 5–13, for instance, placed directly after the poem of vv. 2–3 to offer the strongest possible contrast.

> What wrong did your ancestors find in me
>   that they went far from me,
>   and went after worthless things, and became worthless
>   themselves?
> They did not say, "Where is the Lord
>   who brought us up from the land of Egypt,
> who led us in the wilderness,
>   in a land of deserts and pits,
> in a land of drought and deep darkness,
>   in a land that no one passes through,
>   where no one lives?"
> And I brought you into a plentiful land .
>   to eat its fruits and its good things.
> But when you entered you defiled my land,
>   and made my heritage an abomination.
> The priests did not say, "Where is the Lord?"
>   Those who handle the law did not know me;
> the rulers transgressed against me;
> the prophets prophesied by Baal,
>   and went after things that do not profit.
>
> Therefore once more I accuse you,
>   says the Lord,
>   and I accuse your children's children.
> Cross to the coasts of Cyprus and look,
>   send to Kedar and examine with care;
>   see if there has ever been such a thing.
> Has a nation changed its gods,
>   even though they are no gods?

But my people have changed their glory
   for something that does not profit.
Be appalled, O heavens, at this,
   be shocked, be utterly desolate,
     says the Lord,
for my people have committed two evils:
   they have forsaken me,
   the fountain of living water,
and dug out cisterns for themselves,
   cracked cisterns,
   that can hold no water.

                              (2:5–13, NRSV)

This poem does not need the detailed comment that 2:2–3 did. We can easily follow the course of Jeremiah's rhetoric. But there are a few details that we may note.

Look at v. 5:

What wrong did your ancestors find in me
   that they went far from me,
   and went after worthless things, and became worthless
     themselves?

There is a poignancy about the first two lines. The tone is almost like that of a hurt lover saying, Sweetheart, what did I do wrong? Many of us have grown up visualizing the God of the Old Testament as a deity with a white beard, sitting on a throne in heaven, smiting people. We think that it is only in the New Testament, from Jesus, that we hear of a God of love. One could question whether Jesus' words are always so reassuring (see, e.g., Luke 6:24–26; 17:2). And one can definitely question any such assumption about the Old Testament in the light of a passage such as this. Imagine, God the hurt lover! Now it is true that this question of Yahweh's in 2:5 is a rhetorical question—the situation is more that of a public trial in which Yahweh is indicting Israel for breach of contract (see esp. v. 9 below). But for Yahweh even to open the legal argument with Israel by saying, For the record, did I do anything wrong? is to suggest in an extraordinary way the possibility of dialogue between Yahweh and the people. The Old Testament constantly stretches us beyond our conventional religious notions, never more than in the book of Jeremiah.

In v. 5 the words "worthless things" and "worthless" represent the same Hebrew word *(hebel)* that begins the book of Ecclesiastes (translated there "vanity"). Evidently the word originally indicated "hot air" or "smoke"—that which is insubstantial, that which has no solidity. Jeremiah uses the term here to refer to pagan gods, but he is calling them "hot-air gods" not only to ridicule their undependability but also because the word he uses sounds a bit like "Baal," the designation for the fertility god to which many of the people were devoted.

It is worthwhile to note also that the verb "went," which we see twice in v. 5, is the same Hebrew verb that is translated as "followed" in v. 2; this identity of wording is concealed by the English translation. Israel once walked after Yahweh in the wilderness; since then Israel has walked after hot-air gods.

Fertility Worship: Quid pro Quo

One of the most difficult aspects of Old Testament life to understand is the attraction of fertility worship. How was it that thoughtful people could turn away from the worship of the God of Genesis and Exodus to gods and goddesses whose worship demanded cultic prostitution and drunkenness?

We must remind ourselves that this was an age without financial guarantees or security. Personal holdings were in land, in houses, in a few household possessions—but most of all in herds, flocks, and harvest. Those herds, flocks, and harvests represented the margin between family prosperity and starvation, and a healthy number of sons and daughters represented one's social security for old age (imagine the fearful infant mortality rate of those times). Hence much of one's security in the community was dependent upon the fertility of fields and livestock and upon one's own fertility as well.

Palestine is largely unsuited to irrigation, that hedge against drought; and rainfall, though it usually comes, tends to be spotty. No wonder the Canaanites who lived on the land had developed fertility worship to a high art, and no wonder, too, that the Israelites, as they themselves settled into agriculture, tended to adopt the Canaanite concerns and rituals. The God whom the Israelites called Yahweh had been understood to be a God who had protected them (2:3 implied it, we noticed).

But "baal" means nothing more than "lord" or "owner"; there was a divine "baal" for this field, another for that river, and still another for the spring yonder. Baal, then, was an all-purpose term, and there must have been a good deal of blending of the worship of Yahweh and of Baal (Who knows? the Israelites must have thought; perhaps Baal is simply another name for Yahweh after all!). So it was that King Saul could name one of his sons Eshbaal, roughly translated as "man of Baal" (1 Chron. 8:33; the form in 2 Sam. 2:8, Ishboshesh, is a censored version of the name). We are not to assume that King Saul *worshiped* Baal rather than Yahweh, but simply that he casually *identified* the two. This seems to be the burden of Elijah's challenge to Israel about 850 B.C.E. (1 Kings 18:21): the two deities are different; you must choose. But so frantic was the search and need for fertility that it must have been very difficult to give up these practices. No Baal image, so far as I know, has as yet been unearthed in Palestine from any Israelite period, but dozens of little figurines of Astarte, the goddess of fertility, have been dug up; women must have been particularly prone to such worship (see the discussion in chap. XI on 44:15).

High in the Lebanese mountains is a lovely site called Afqa. Near there the Ibrahim River emerges out of a cavern in the mountains and makes its way down through steep valleys until it flows into the Mediterranean Sea, just south of the old Phoenician port of Byblos. It is clear from both archaeological evidence and ancient authors that Byblos was a center for fertility worship. So, too, was that site high in the mountains where the river flows out of the cavern; its greater flow in the spring was the sign to the worshipers that Baal had renewed his lease on life for the coming year. It is an extraordinary place, spooky inside the cavern, truly a fit place for the worship of the forces of nature. Across from the entrance to the cavern are the foundations of an ancient temple to Astarte, the fertility goddess—it must have been an imposing structure in its time—and by one corner of the foundation there remains today the stump of an old tree, from which new-sprouting twigs still grow. To these twigs are tied white strips of cloth torn from the garments of ill or barren women in the villages of the region; both Orthodox Christian and Muslim women resort to the practice. Next to the stump is a small shrine, with a crude icon of the Virgin Mary inside; the first time I visited the spot and looked into the shrine, a candle was burning. For at least fifteen hundred years the temple has been in ruins, and it is the Virgin Mary rather than Astarte who has been venerated; yet the prayers offered up at the spot are plainly still the same. Such is the everlasting, understandable hunger for health and children, and such must have been the passion of the Israelites in the days when Jeremiah preached.

Well, we might wonder, this is all very natural; what is so harmful about it? In days before medical science, in days before public and private agencies organized help for the helpless of society, what was so harmful about fertility worship?

The major problem, as the prophets saw it, was not necessarily in the excesses of sexuality and drunkenness in the cultic celebrations, though this was certainly an aspect of the problem. Far worse was that in people's minds the Baals tended, so to speak, to be cosmic servants, ready to grant wishes to the people if only the people offered them adequate tips; whereas Yahweh, the God of the covenant, would grant the blessings of fertility to a people who remained sensitive to the expectations of ethical behavior in the covenant.[1]

Yahweh deals with the people not on a quid pro quo basis but on the basis of grace and mercy, in response to the sensitivity that Yahweh's people manifest to Yahweh's will. In short, what was at stake in this issue of the worship of the Baals versus the worship of Yahweh was the nature of the relationship between the people and the deity. People tended to think of the Baals as transactional gods whose main job was giving rewards or prizes, and to forget questions of the quality of life altogether.

All this is implied by the warm, sad words of Yahweh in Jer. 2:5.

Jeremiah 2:6–13

Verse 6 characterizes Yahweh more closely as the God of the exodus out of Egypt. It is curious that we tend to feel that the specificity of such a "creed" is limiting. We want our creeds to be general, and so we talk first about God in creation: "I believe in God the Father Almighty, maker of heaven and earth," we begin. Israel, however, always began with the specificity of the act of rescue out of Egypt, never with the generality of creation. Think of the beginning of the Ten Commandments: "I am the Lord your God, who brought you out of the land of Egypt, out of the house of bondage" (Exod. 20:2). Israel always began there.

The Old Testament people seemed to sense that creation is not a secure way to begin to characterize God, since creation has within it not only the glories of sunset and stars, the marvels of life together in families, but the terrors of earthquake and the fearful death of plague as well. Beginning their story with the rescue from Egypt announced right away that God is a God of grace and mercy, a God who is *more gracious* than we expect. Look at the way the nightmarish descriptions of the desert pile up in this verse. Who would want to linger in a land where the darkness is appalling, in a land in which no one lives? (You and I, in our crowded world, crave solitude often; not so the Israelites, who craved company and the security of the village and town above all!) And Yahweh led Israel even through the wilderness.

Verse 7 brings a contrast—the lovely land, the plentiful land, literally a land of orchards, a land the people, according to the accusation, polluted and made unclean. And the leadership— priests and prophets—is very much to blame (v. 8).

The situation is clear: Israel has turned its back on Yahweh and Yahweh's gracious acts and has gone off instead after fertility gods. So now Yahweh delivers an indictment. For it is an indictment here, as the legal language of v. 9 makes clear. "Accuse" in Hebrew really means "call to law, indict, sue." If the ancestors went astray (v. 5), then God in return indicts even the grandchildren (v. 9). For go to the far northwest to the island of Cyprus, or to the far southeast, to the Arab tribe of Kedar: has there ever been a precedent for a nation's switching gods (v. 10)? Why, the pagan nations are more loyal to their nonexistent gods than Israel is to the true God—what irony this is! (v. 11).

Then comes the summary to the witnesses (the heavens, in v. 12, function in this cosmic law-court scene as a kind of jury). The summary begins: my people have abandoned me (v. 13), the spring that always gives forth running water, and have resorted instead to cisterns dug out of the soft limestone and prepared to catch the rainwater. Now, a cistern that stores water is by no means the equivalent of a spring that produces water on its own, but even so, it may suffice—unless it leaks, as these cisterns do. Here is a perfect summary image of the uselessness of the Baal gods: not only do they not produce the water needed to ensure fertility, they suck dry even the water that is collected there! We should remind ourselves here how precious water is in a dry and thirsty land (cf. Psalm 63:1). To be out on a summer walk and to have planned for one's noon destination a spot where there has been water in the past, only to find there no water at all by which to slake one's thirst can be a fatal mistake; one can go without food for many days, but not water. And in a land where water cannot always be depended on, Jeremiah's contrast between the dependable spring and the cracked cisterns is a telling climax to this poem.

A Possible Date for 2:1–13

What might the occasion have been for Jeremiah's speaking out this sequence of poetry in 2:1–13? When and where might this message have been delivered? The text itself obviously does not say, so we are left to ponder possibilities. We have presumed that there was a resurgence of Baal worship during the reign of King Jehoiakim, and it also seems likely that the material in chapters 2 and 3 was delivered early in Jeremiah's career.

Let me make a suggestion. Jeremiah 2:2 begins, "Go and proclaim in the hearing of Jerusalem" (lit. "Go and call out in the ears of Jerusalem"). Deuteronomy 31:11 ends, "You shall read this law before all Israel in their hearing" (lit. "You shall call out this law before all Israel in their ears"). Deuteronomy 31:10–13, remember, gives the instructions for the reading of the law of Deuteronomy every seven years (see chap. II). If the law of Deuteronomy was first publicized in 622 B.C.E., then the first such repetition would be at the feast of booths in 615 B.C.E. (see chap. II). The next repetition would be at the feast of booths in 608 B.C.E., about a year after King Jehoiakim was put on the throne. I have already suggested that the "harvest" mentioned in v. 3 suggests the vintage harvest, and there is an early association between the feast of booths and both the vintage harvest (see Deut. 16:13) and the exodus from Egypt (see Lev. 23:39, 43). A plausible setting for these words would then be the feast of booths in the fall of 608

B.C.E., on the occasion of the rereading of Deuteronomy. It is useful for us to ponder the effect of these words in such a context.

One other question may be touched on at this point: Why are Jeremiah's words in the sermon at the Temple (7:1–12) in *prose*, yet these words in chapter 2 in *poetry*? The simple answer is, we do not know. Jeremiah may have delivered the Temple Sermon in poetic form, only to have it summarized in prose form in the tradition. Or he may have delivered the Temple Sermon deliberately in the style of legal prose in order to underline how important it was for the people to adhere to torah, the law. Or it may be that he delivered the Temple Sermon in prose and found his poetic voice only some months later. After all, the tradition attributed to Moses contained both prose (the core of Deuteronomy in the scroll brought to King Josiah) and poetry (it seems clear that the long poem in Deuteronomy 32, "The Song of Moses," was known and imitated by Jeremiah). If Jeremiah was to be the prophet like Moses, he could offer words from God in both prose and poetry, as he understood Moses to have done.

Jeremiah 2:14–37

Other poems, Jer. 2:14–19, 20–25, 26–28, and 29–37, continue the themes of Yahweh's disappointment in Israel's unfaithfulness, and it is not hard to follow their imagery. A few remarks will suffice here. In contrast to the honeymoon days of Israel, when other nations that attacked Israel were defeated (v. 3), now the foreign nations feel free to attack, just as a lion roars confidently over his prey (vv. 14–15). Egypt in particular has humiliated Judah (Memphis and Tahpanhes in v. 16 are Egyptian cities). And, continuing the water image of v. 13, since the cracked cisterns have not satisfied Judah's thirst, Judah has gone off alternately to drink the water of Egypt or of Assyria, that is, to seek foreign aid (v. 18). The mention of Assyria is doubtless a poetic designation of whatever power is currently in control in Mesopotamia—now Babylon.

Verses 20–25 explore in great detail the image of Israel as harlot. What is meant here is not only the actual prostitution that occurred during the fertility ceremonies but more particularly the figurative prostitution of Israel's adherence to the Baal gods rather than to the true Lord, Yahweh. "You sprawled and played the whore" (v. 20, NRSV) is a truer translation than "You bowed down as a harlot" (RSV). The vine image in v. 21 picks up the "first fruits" image of 2:3, reflecting the picture of Israel as the vineyard of God which was earlier set forth in Isa. 5:1–7. And the stain image of v. 22 echoes Isaiah's words in Isa. 1:15–17. Each prophet took it for granted that his hearers had their ears full of the pronouncements of earlier prophets; it is difficult for us always to catch previous references in these later expressions. This is why it is true that the more one reads in biblical material, the better one understands whatever text is being read.

The animal imagery in 2:23–24 provides a good example of how misunderstandings can creep into commentaries and even into translations of the Bible. Scholars have assumed that both the camel and the wild ass described here are female animals in heat, and several commentators have deleted the reference to the wild ass as a presumably unauthentic addition to the text that overloads the poetry and spoils the original sequence of ideas that Jeremiah intended; the Jerusalem Bible (JB) and the New English Bible (NEB) have followed this assumption. On the other hand, the New Jerusalem Bible (NJB) has omitted the camel!

Some years ago, however, my colleague Kenneth E. Bailey, who had lived and worked for many years in rural Egypt, remarked that the commentators simply do not understand how these animals actually behave. About the phrase "a restive young camel, interlacing her tracks," he explained that the female camel does not experience sexual heat; she is quite casual when the male seeks her out. The point of the camel image here is that the camel is young, and young camels cannot walk straight; when a young camel gets loose in the marketplace, everyone scrambles out of the way, because no one knows where the camel will step next. The female wild ass, however, is another story. When her season is upon her, she is frantic for the male and seeks to track him down by the scent of the urine that he has deposited. When she picks up the scent, she goes frantic with joy and races off to find the mate. Thus, "A wild ass . . . in her heat sniffing the wind! Who can restrain her lust?" The young camel cannot walk straight, while the female wild ass in heat cannot be diverted from racing straight to her sexual goal. The point is that neither of these animals is particularly "responsible," and both are equally striking images for Judah gone astray. Hence the lines about both animals belong in the text.

Notice also the words that Yahweh puts in the mouth of Judah. Before the words about the animals, Yahweh accuses Judah, saying, "How can you say, 'I am not defiled, I have not gone after the Baals'?" (v. 23). Yahweh accuses Judah of denying any accusations—Who me? I don't know what you're talking about! (v. 23). But then after the words about the animals, Yahweh understands Judah to yield to the accusation, but without any remorse: "It is hopeless, for I have loved strangers, and after them I will go" (v. 25; cf. "go after" and "went after" in v. 5). Israel figuratively shrugs its shoulders at Yahweh, unwilling to take any responsibility.

In v. 27 Jeremiah seems to have switched the sex references ironically; a leafy tree, after all, is a suitable symbol of female fertility, and a standing stone of male fertility, rather than as Jeremiah gives them. That he should identify the sex references wrongly is evidence of his mockery of the fertility gods.

The Greek text (the Septuagint) has preserved two lines in v. 28 that have unfortunately dropped out of the traditional Hebrew text. The last part of the verse should evidently read:

> For as many as your cities
> are your gods, O Judah,
> *and as many as your streets, O Jerusalem,*
> *have they sacrificed to Baal.*
>
> (italics added)

The closing verses of the chapter continue many of the images and themes with which we have already become familiar; there is, it seems, nothing ahead for Judah but humiliation (vv. 36–37).

Jeremiah 3:1—4:4

Chapter 3 begins with a fresh series of poems on the theme of Judah's disloyalty. The chapter is interrupted by two sections of prose (3:6–11, 16–18) that, by their contrasting styles, give evidence of being added to the poetic material at a later stage in the building up of the book of Jeremiah; when those two sections are put aside, four poems are left: vv. 1–5, 12b–15, 19–20, and 21–25. Though these poems, as I have indicated, continue the theme of harlotry, there is a new note: these poems are united by the Hebrew verb *shûb*, translated variously as "turn" or "return," which Jeremiah employs in a wide range of meanings.

In chapter 3 we find two images of Israel intermixed: (1) the image of Israel as the "wife" of Yahweh, an image we have already met in 2:2–3 and by implication in other passages of chapter 2; and (2) the image of the people of Israel as the "children" or "sons" of Yahweh. Thus 3:1 contains the image of husband and wife, as in chapter 2. Then, according to v. 19, we hear that Israel should call Yahweh "my father" (the same phrase occurs in v. 4, though I suspect that the original reading was different).[2] And then in v. 20, as in v. 1, the image reverts to that of husband and wife. Both images are derived from the prophet Hosea a hundred years before. Hosea 1—3 sets forth the image of Israel as wife to Yahweh; in Hosea 11:1–9 the image is that of sonship. The prophet Ezekiel solves the tension later by his allegory in Ezekiel 16 of Israel as the foundling baby girl, exposed to die but adopted by Yahweh as his daughter and then espoused to him as his bride when she came of age. For the moment we can only say that both images occur, and the seeming inconsistency did not worry Jeremiah. The point is simple. The basic question is, To whom does Israel belong? In that patriarchal society, a wife belonged to her husband, and children belonged to their father. The specific relationship is of secondary importance, but identifying to whom Israel belongs is all important.

Jeremiah 3:1 deals with a common domestic legal situation: "If a man divorces his wife and she goes from him and becomes another man's wife, will he return to her?" But Jeremiah's second question—"Would not that land be greatly polluted?"—leaves us puzzled; its logic escapes us. And it evidently escaped the translator of the Septuagint Greek as well, because that text gives the question as "Would not that *woman* be greatly polluted?" a translation also used in the NEB. But the Hebrew text is evidently correct after all; Jeremiah meant "land." He was thinking of the law in Deut. 24:1–4, whereby the land incurs guilt when a former husband takes back a wife who has belonged to another man. The point made here in Jeremiah is that Judah has done something seemingly irrevocable; if Judah expects Yahweh to take Judah back, it is expecting Yahweh to break Yahweh's own torah!

The rest of the poem in vv. 1–5 is clear, although two things might be noted about v. 2. First, the Hebrew verb translated "been lain with" was evidently considered in such poor taste in ancient times that a less offensive verb has always been substituted for it in the public reading of the Hebrew scriptures; even "been ravished" (NEB) or "offered your sex" (NJB) are not as strong as the Hebrew word was. Second, the reference to "an Arab in the wilderness" sounds offensive today. One is tempted, on first reading, to assume that Jeremiah was making a disparaging remark about the lustfulness of Arabs, but he had in mind, rather, the image of Bedouins who lived by raiding, waiting to waylay a caravan.

Verse 3 interrupts the continuity between vv. 2 and 4. I believe it is a verse added by Jeremiah later, after the onset of the great drought. I shall discuss this in detail in chapter VI.

In 3:14 we find the phrase "for I am your master," and in 3:24 the phrase "the shameful thing has devoured." Both phrases mask references to Baal. In v. 14, Jeremiah has used a verb derived from the noun "baal"—"I have 'lorded' you," which means something like "I have been your (real) 'Baal.'" Remember the word "baal" simply means "lord" or "owner." It is as if Yahweh is saying, One master is *not* like another; you have one true master, and the rest are false. So do not seek after the Baal gods; the title "Baal" really belongs to me, to Yahweh. (Jeremiah uses the same verb once more, in 31:32; see chap. X.)

In v. 24, the Hebrew word *bōsheth*, which really means "shame," was the standard euphemism for "Baal." Earlier I noted that one of Saul's sons was named Eshbaal (1 Chron. 8:33), but the form recorded in 2 Sam. 2:8 was Ishbosheth, which I called a censored version of the name, with the euphemism "bosheth" substituted for "baal" in the name. Jeremiah uses the euphemism here in 3:24 because he is anticipating the phrase "let us lie down in our *shame*" in v. 25. In every way he can, then, he is exploring the whole matter of the false relationship between Israel and the Baal gods, and the true relationship between Israel and Yahweh which the nation has rejected.

Chapter 2 began with the poignant question of the hurt lover, "What wrong did your fathers find in me?" (v. 5). Chapter 3 voices Yahweh's appeal for the kind of genuine repentance Yahweh would like to see Israel manifest.

> Return, faithless Israel. . . . Only acknowledge your guilt."
> (vv. 12, 13)
> Return, O faithless children, I will heal your faithlessness. (v. 22)

I mentioned earlier that this chapter works on the various meanings of "turn" or "return." But no English translation can communicate the piling up of words related to "turn" in these passages; in that last phrase, the Hebrew sounds something like "Return, turnable children, and I will heal your turnings." How strange that Israel should find it so easy to turn away from Yahweh and so hard to turn back!

Finally, in 4:1–4, Jeremiah spells out the basic requirements of returning to Yahweh—sincerity, truth-telling. If Israel can embrace these, Israel will become what Yahweh expected the nation to be in the promise to Abraham in Gen. 12:2—a blessing to the other nations of the world (v. 2). There is even Scripture to guide Israel; v. 3 is a reference to Hosea 10:12, and v. 4 a reference to Deut. 10:16.

One final question lingers. Does the imagery of these poems, heavy with sexuality as it is, really communicate the situation of faith to a modern reader, or does such imagery perhaps prove so offensive that it is unable to speak of the things of faith? Many people go to the Bible for a higher vision than the world affords, for lofty vistas that draw them out of the shabbiness of day-to-day living. To them, the blunt language of Jeremiah may seem unattractive at best, a stumbling block at worst. What can we say to this?

Much, but this at least: the biblical faith never claims to take people out from the world but testifies, in fact, to a God who enters our world, loves it, testifies that Jesus Christ went to the cross for it. The biblical faith does not emphasize a "spiritual" part of humankind at all but sees us whole, our cravings and hungers and lusts as well as our ideals and hopes and dreams. The Bible speaks of our "knowing" God, and of God's "knowing" us. "Knowing," in the Old Testament, however, is not factual acquaintance with but rather intimate relationship with; we may notice the striking use of "know" in Gen. 4:1 to refer to sexual relations. If biblical knowledge is symbolized by the relation of the marriage bed, then marriage-gone-wrong is a vivid picture to put in contrast to marriage-which-should-go-right. Hosea's language seems like that of a rural person who minces no words (Hosea 2:2–5); Jeremiah uses some of the same sexual imagery, but with far greater warmth and lyricism. This is why we have been speaking of God as the hurt lover.

Perhaps the point is best made in the phrasing of 2:27: "For they have turned their backs to me, and not their faces." "Backs" here translates a Hebrew word (*'ōreph*) meaning "the back of the neck." In Exod. 32:9 the people are called "stiff-necked," using the same word: the back of their neck is stiff; they are stubborn. So here in Jeremiah, the prophet perceives Yahweh to be saying, The people have turned the back of the neck to me rather than their face. How can Yahweh carry on a conversation with the back of a neck? How can Yahweh bring Israel to the point of turning around once more, saying, I'm sorry, and reembarking on the great relationship with Yahweh? What kind of God is this, who is desolate that this great project has gone astray, who is baffled by such stubbornness? What can Yahweh do?

Next we shall have to explore Jeremiah's sense of what God can do.

NOTES

1. For further portrayals of the struggle between the worship of the Baals and the worship of Yahweh, see Hosea 2:4–8. "Their mother" in v. 4 is a figure for Israel; "lovers" in v. 5 represents the Baal gods; and "my first husband" is of course Yahweh. Or see Deut. 28:1–6.

2. By my analysis "my father" in v. 4 is a later gloss (explanation of a copyist) and the first line of the verse originally read, "Is not 'my mainstay' what you have called me?" For this analysis see my *Jeremiah 1*, Hermeneia (Philadelphia: Fortress Press, 1986), 58, 115.

**GOD PLANS WAR
ON JUDAH, AND JEREMIAH
DICTATES A SCROLL**

The next large section of the poetry of Jeremiah begins at 4:5 and continues, with several interruptions, through chapter 10. The theme of this material is not the harlotry of the people but the coming of an enemy army from the north to destroy the covenant people. In this chapter we will examine some of the poetry in chapters 4 and 6, but before we do so we must take account of three matters. The first is an important historical event that lies in the background, the Battle of Carchemish in 605 B.C.E.; the second is Jeremiah's visit to the potter in 18:1–12; and the third is the matter of Jeremiah's dictating a scroll in 36:1–8, an event that likewise took place in 605 B.C.E.

The Battle of Carchemish:
Jeremiah 46:3–12

I noted in chapter III that Egypt had not achieved a definitive victory against the Babylonians at Haran in the campaign of 609 B.C.E. Over the next four years the Babylonians tried unsuccessfully to secure positions near Carchemish to dislodge the Egyptians. Then, in the early summer of 605 B.C.E., Nebuchadrezzar, the son of the Babylonian king, dealt a stunning defeat to the Egyptian forces at Carchemish, after which he pursued them south and defeated them again at Hamath in Syria (the modern Hama, 120 miles north of Damascus). In August of the same year, having received news of the death of his father, Nebuchadrezzar returned to Babylon to assume the crown.

Suddenly Egypt was no longer a power. Indeed, at the end of the following year, 604 B.C.E., the Babylonian army marched down the coast of Palestine and destroyed the city of Ashkelon, the last remaining stronghold of the Philistines—a scant forty miles west of Jerusalem. Seemingly overnight Babylon had replaced Egypt as the great power in the region. Soon Jehoiakim would be forced to switch sides and become a vassal to Babylon (2 Kings 24:1). One wonders whether 2:18 and 2:36 refer to this shift in the king's loyalty; those verses certainly fit such circumstances!

Jeremiah 46:3–12 is a poem in which Jeremiah mocks the weakness of the Egyptian army in the battle of Carchemish. I suggest that in vv. 3–8 the Babylonians are being addressed. While the Babylonians had cavalry units, the Egyptians used war horses only with chariots. So a battle order to the Babylonians to "mount, O horsemen" could only panic the Egyptians. Indeed "they" (the Egyptians) have turned backward (v. 5) from the great battle in the north (v. 6). Egypt had thought that, like its river the Nile, it would rise and cover the earth (v. 8). But, as everybody knows, as the Nile rises, it must also fall; and Egypt has surely fallen.

Verse 9 contains battle orders to the Egyptians. The orders to advance,

Advance, O horses, and rage, O chariots! Let the warriors go forth

can in Hebrew just as well be heard as orders to *flee* the battle:

Rear up, O horses, and run wild, O chariots! Let the warriors leave [the battle].

Verse 11 suggests that Egypt should go off to Gilead, east of the Jordan, to get unguent for its wounds.

Of course this poem of Jeremiah's only symbolically addresses Babylon and Egypt. The prophet had no direct access at that time to the Babylonians or Egyptians, and the audience for the poem would have been his fellow citizens in Judah. We have already discussed the scathing oracle he had delivered against Jehoiakim's building project (Jer. 22:13–19; see chap. III); now here is a poem that mocks the prowess of the nation that had put King Jehoiakim on the throne in the first place!

Jeremiah's Visit to the Potter: Jeremiah 18:1–12

This has become one of the notable passages in Jeremiah: the metaphor that God is the potter and we are the clay is a congenial one for us. But in the ease of the metaphor, some of the nuances of the event may have been missed.

Jeremiah visits the workshop of a potter, the narrative says, at Yahweh's behest. There he watches the potter shaping a pot on his wheel; the pot is not emerging satisfactorily, so the potter presses down the lump of clay to start again.

To Jeremiah this is a metaphor for Yahweh's work with nations. But the key word comes toward the beginning of vv. 7 and 9. In Hebrew the word is *rega'*; in the NRSV it is translated as both "at one moment," and "at another moment"; but it actually means "suddenly." If, when Yahweh intends to do destructive work against a particular nation, that nation changes its ways for the better, then Yahweh will suddenly cancel all plans for evil toward that nation. And if, when Yahweh intends to do constructive work with a particular nation, that nation changes its ways for the worse, then Yahweh will suddenly cancel plans for good works toward that nation. Yahweh is sovereign and can change plans:

Am I not able to do with you, house of Israel, like this potter? (v. 6).

It is clear, then, that Yahweh is not locked into a given attitude toward any particular nation. In 609 B.C.E., at Haran, Egypt was supreme; in 605 B.C.E., after the Battles of Carchemish and Hamath, Babylon is on top and Egypt on the bottom. All this is Yahweh's doing. If Yahweh intends disaster against Judah, and Judah repents, then Yahweh can intend good things for Judah. How will Judah respond?

Jeremiah Dictates a Scroll

In 36:1–8 there is a narrative about a scroll that Jeremiah was called to dictate in 605 B.C.E., and this, too, is important background for our understanding of some of the poems in chapters 4 and 6. The time was the fourth year of Jehoiakim (36:1), that is, the year from the spring of 605 B.C.E. to the spring of 604 B.C.E., the year in which the Babylonians defeated the Egyptians at Carchemish and Hamath.

Two reasons are given for Jeremiah's dictating a scroll instead of speaking at the Temple. The first and more immediate is that he was "debarred" or "restricted" from the Temple (36:5). Thus if he could not directly communicate his prophetic words, he at least wanted to make sure that they were communicated indirectly. The narrative does not say why he was restricted from the Temple, but if he had been reciting poems such as the one mocking Egypt (46:3–12), it is easy to see why he would have been persona non grata in the Temple area. So Jeremiah takes on a scribe, Baruch the son of Neriah. Baruch is to take the scroll that Jeremiah has dictated to him and read it in the temple on a fast day (36:6) "in the hearing of all the people": one may assume that it was on the Day of Atonement (Yom Kippur) late in September or early in October in 605 B.C.E.

The second and ultimate reason for the dictation of the scroll is to warn the people, so that they might have an opportunity to repent. Thus Jeremiah understands Yahweh to say,

> It may be that the house of Judah will hear all the evil which I intend to do to them, so that every one may turn from his evil way, and that I may forgive their iniquity and their sin. (36:3)

And so Jeremiah tells Baruch,

> It may be that their supplication will come before the Lord, and that every one will turn from his evil way, for great is the anger and wrath that the Lord has pronounced against this people. (36:7)

The words of the scroll will include words of warning of potential disaster ahead, so that people might have the opportunity to change their ways before it is too late.

The Contents of the Original Scroll

It is tempting to try to imagine the precise contents of this first scroll that Jeremiah dictated. There is no way to know for sure, of course, but one may make some educated guesses. One assumes that there must have been some version of Jeremiah's call, such as is now found in chapter 1, since Jeremiah found himself challenged more than once during his prophetic activity (cf. chap. III). The material in 2:1—4:4, as we established in chapter IV, consists largely of Yahweh's *accusations* of Israel's disloyalty, while the material in 4:5—10:25 consists largely of Yahweh's announcement of *punishment* of the people by means of the coming of an enemy from the north, punishment appropriate to Israel's disloyalty. If the contents of the scroll are to warn the people so that they have an opportunity to repent, then various portions of the accusation section (including the appeals to repentance in 3:12, 14, 22) and various portions of the punishment section are appropriate. I will not try to be more specific about what portions of 2:1—4:4 might have been included, but it becomes important to try to discern what portions of the punishment sections were included, as we shall see in a moment.

Jeremiah 4:5–8, 13–18, 29–31

Let us begin with 4:13–18. This passage not only describes the coming of the enemy from the north (vv. 13, 15–17) but also contains an appeal to the people to change their ways, "O Jerusalem, wash your heart clean of wickedness, so that you may be saved" (v. 14). As such, it fits the purpose of the scroll perfectly—to warn.

Two other poems in this chapter, vv. 5–8 and 29–31, resemble vv. 13–18. This resemblance is based on a striking characteristic: even though all the poems are addressed to the people, each poem contains a comparable pattern of shifts of speaker. Prophetic oracles that offer a shift of speaker are evidently a new phenomenon in the discourse of the prophets; I shall return to the matter later on. For now we must simply identify the speakers, verse by verse.

As for 4:5–8, God is the speaker in vv. 5–7 (we note v. 6, "I bring evil from the north"), but Jeremiah is the speaker in v. 8: one of the tasks of the prophet is to summon people to repentance. And there is another twist in v. 8; the NRSV translates correctly,

Because of this put on sackcloth, lament and wail: "The fierce anger of the Lord has not turned away from us."

That is, the last half of the verse is not the *reason* for lament, as most translations have it, including the RSV; it is, rather, the *content* of the lament that Jeremiah is giving to the *people* to recite.

The sequence of speakers is identical in 4:29–31: Yahweh speaks in vv. 29–30, and then in v. 31 Jeremiah speaks, ending with a quotation of the people.

Verses 13–18 offer a more complex scheme: Yahweh speaks in the first three lines of v. 13, only to be interrupted by a cry of the people in the fourth line. Jeremiah speaks to the people in v. 14, appealing to the city to repent. Yahweh resumes speaking in vv. 15–17, and Jeremiah evidently summarizes the situation in v. 18. A diagram will make the matter clear. (See Figure 1.)

vv. 5–7:	Yahweh	vv. 29–30:	Yahweh
v. 8:	Jeremiah, with quotation of people	v. 31:	Jeremiah, with quotation of people

	v. 13:	Yahweh; last line: people
	v. 14:	Jeremiah
	vv. 15–17	Yahweh
	v. 18:	Jeremiah

Figure 1

Now, finally, we can look at the content of these poems, beginning with 4:5–8. Yahweh speaks. The functional equivalent today of the first line of his announcement in v. 5 would be, "Sound the air-raid sirens through the land." The contrast between a city and a village in those days was not size, though that inevitably entered into the picture. The contrast actually lay in defense walls—a city had them, the surrounding villages did not. The consequence, then, was that whenever an invading army approached, the signal would be given, and the farmers and tradesmen would drop their work on the spot, gather up their wives and children and servants, and make for the city, hoping that they could all get into the city before the gates were closed and barred, and hoping, too, that the city fathers had made adequate provision for food and water within the city for the duration of the siege. (Cf. the similar images of impending disaster and its impact on the villagers in Mark 13:14–18.) Sieges in ancient times could last a long time; Nebuchadrezzar besieged the Phoenician city of Tyre for thirteen years before the city acknowledged Babylonian sovereignty! And Jerusalem itself in its final besieging by Nebuchadrezzar would hold out for a year and a half, from approximately January 588 to July 587 B.C.E. (see chap. XI).

The "lion" in v. 7 is an old image for the invader from Mesopotamia. It has already occurred in 2:15, and Isaiah had used it a hundred years before (Isa. 5:26–30). The result of the invasion will be that the land will become "a waste" and the cities uninhabitable. But since the signal has been sounded through the land and the people have streamed to the cities for refuge (v. 5), it is ominous to be told that those refuges themselves will become uninhabitable!

The identity of the enemy, as I have already suggested, is Babylon. One might object that Babylon is not north of Jerusalem at all, but east. On a map of the whole Middle East this is true, but Jeremiah was considering the matter from a local perspective. An invader marching to Palestine from Babylon would actually follow a course northwest up the Euphrates River and then leave the river, cutting west across to the city of Aleppo, then straight south through Hamath (Hama) to Damascus, then southwest to meet the Jordan River just north of the Sea of Galilee at the city of Hazor, then south to Jerusalem or else south along the coast of Palestine and east to Jerusalem. But the main thrust of such an invader would be south from Aleppo and Damascus, and this is what Jeremiah had in mind.

Jeremiah may have had something else in mind, too, in mentioning the north. There were old myths in the back of the minds of the Israelites, myths of pagan gods gathering in the far north to plot disaster for people. That northern gathering place of the gods is referred to more than once in the Old Testament: the mythical nation of Gog comes from the uttermost parts of the north (Ezek. 38:15), God's own splendor comes out of the north (Job 37:22), and Psalm 48:2–3 most curiously identifies that gathering place in the north with Zion in Jerusalem, the mountain of Yahweh. The "north" therefore represented a special source of fright to Jeremiah's hearers.

The most important thing about vv. 5–7 is not, however, details of military preparation for siege or the identity of the besieger.

Rather, it is the portrayal of Yahweh taking action against the people, actually initiating the process by which the invader is coming. It is not even that Yahweh has *allowed* the invader to slip in. No, Yahweh *summons* the invader to come and lay waste the land. Recall, now, that the whole understanding of Israel's covenant was that Yahweh would defend Israel against its enemies and defeat them (2:3), in fact, that Yahweh would lead Israel in holy war (cf. Exod. 15:3: "The Lord is a man of war"). Now, suddenly, because Israel has broken the covenant with Yahweh, Yahweh has declared holy war *against* Israel. Israel is now the enemy of Yahweh. It might be possible for Israel to handle a human enemy, one even so awesome as Babylon; but to be opposed by Yahweh, who brings on, who sponsors, an enemy, is to be caught in a one-sided fight indeed. No wonder Jeremiah urges the people to lamentation and wailing, urges them to cry, "The fierce anger of the Lord has not turned away from us" (v. 8).

Let us now turn to vv. 13–18. With v. 13 Yahweh once more speaks in fresh images of the battle to come, and the people respond once more in lament. As we have already seen, Jeremiah interjects an appeal to repentance (cf. v. 8). And once again Yahweh describes the approaching enemy (vv. 15–17), and Jeremiah offers interpretation (v. 18).

In the third poem, 4:29–31, Yahweh speaks in vv. 29 and 30. It is possible that the first line should be translated, "At the shout, 'Horseman and archer!' every town takes to flight," the cry "Horseman and archer!" being the wail of the people in panic. There are two points about v. 29 to note. First, "horseman and archer" evidently refers to the warriors in a war-chariot. The Babylonians did have cavalry units (evidently composed of specially trained tribal people), but the difficulties faced by a cavalryman in controlling his horse and at the same time using a bow and arrow made it easier to use the horse in chariotry. Mesopotamian bas-reliefs show a span of two or three horses drawing the war-chariot; one man holds the reins of the horses, another is the bowman (thus "horseman and archer").

My second point involves the shout in v. 5 to get into the safety of the cities as the invader approaches. We now hear that the towns are forsaken, a reinforcement of the word in v. 7 that the cities will be in ruins. Clearly, in the swirl of battle all order has broken down. In v. 30 God contemptuously addresses the land as if it is a prostitute attracting customers; Jeremiah's contrasting metaphor for the land (v. 31) is of a woman bearing her first child, moaning, "Woe is me," just as the people moaned, "Woe to us" in v. 13.

As I noted earlier, the scroll that Jeremiah dictated to Baruch contained warnings from God, so that people might have a chance to change their ways. That is, all these vivid scenarios of war, siege, and civilian panic are not *predictions* of the future, they are for the moment simply *plans*, not necessarily what God *will* do, but what God *can* do. Notice the operative phrase in 36:3, "all the evil I have in mind to do to them" (NAB). (The other sequences in the chapter, vv. 9–12 and 19–28, seem to come from several years later; I deal with them in chap. VII.)

Jeremiah 6:1–8

One other poem fits the purpose of Jeremiah's first scroll, and that is 6:1–8. Here again, along with a description of the invasion of the foe from the north is a warning from God, an appeal for repentance:

> Take warning, O Jerusalem, or I shall turn from you in disgust, and make you a desolation, an uninhabited land. (6:8, NRSV)

In other passages of chapter 4, we heard Yahweh, Jeremiah, and the people speaking; in 6:4a and 5 we suddenly hear a new voice, the shouts of the enemy. These shouts enclose the moans of the people of Jerusalem (v. 4b) in a striking sequence that uses "noon," "evening," and "night":

> Enemy: Prepare war against her,
> up, and let us attack at noon!
> People: Woe to us, for the day declines,
> the shadows of evening lengthen!
> Enemy: Up, and let us attack by night,
> and destroy her palaces!

These sudden shouts of the enemy raise in our minds two considerations. The first is the powerful effect this kind of prophetic utterance must have had on Jeremiah's audience. We find traces in Micah, a hundred years before, of a kind of dialogue between the prophet and Yahweh, but for Jeremiah to add still other voices must have been astonishing to his hearers.

The second consideration is how Jeremiah signaled these shifts of speaker to his audience. The answer is that we do not fully know. We do not even know how a prophet normally presented his words to an audience. Did he recite them? chant them? sing them? Did he make use of conventions of rhythm, or pace, or gesture that shifted depending on whether he offered the voice of Yahweh or his own voice? What is clear, though, is that there are conventions of phraseology that are appropriate to each speaker. For example, it is clear in the poems we have been examining that (1) Yahweh gives the war news, (2) Jeremiah tries both to mediate between Yahweh and the people and to comment on the scene, and (3) the people utter their wails. These clues help us to reconstruct the sequence of speakers, whatever reinforcing clues of rhythm or tone there might have been in the original performance notwithstanding.

To continue with 6:1–8, Yahweh speaks in vv. 1–3. Verse 1 reminds us of 4:5–6, the sounding of signals to get people to safety. We noted earlier the contradiction between 4:5–6 (villagers should rush to the safety of the city) and 4:29 (everyone should flee the city). Now again in v. 1 Benjaminites are told to flee Jerusalem. Where is there safety? Why are the Benjaminites singled out for mention? Jeremiah comes from the territory of Benjamin, just north of Jerusalem—is this a nod to his kinfolk? Tekoa, by contrast, is south of Jerusalem; it was the home of the prophet Amos (Amos 1:1). There is no safety anywhere.

The Hebrew text of 6:2 is in some disarray: the NRSV translates, "I have likened daughter Zion to the loveliest pasture." By this understanding, Yahweh has treated Jerusalem like a lush pasture—the wording reminds us of 2:7 and 3:19. To this "loveliest pasture" he invites shepherds, shepherds who are not peaceful nomads, however, but foreign invaders bent on conquest. In the language spoken by the Assyrians and Babylonians, "shepherds" could imply "rulers"; it is this double meaning that makes the shouts of the enemy in vv. 4a and 5 so horrifying. Indeed, what kind of enemies are so casual about the taking of a city as to allow half the day to go by before bothering to begin the attack (v. 4a), or so sure of their superiority as to contemplate an attack by darkness (v. 5)? No wonder the people lament that their day is done (v. 4b)!

But the judgment of Yahweh is that Jerusalem keeps its wickedness fresh and available just as much as it keeps its water supply cool and available (v. 7). But wickedness is something the city ought to get rid of rather than keep fresh (recall the appeal to repentance in 4:14). All of this is Yahweh's urgent warning to the people (v. 8).

I have suggested that Jeremiah's first scroll might have included some account of his call in chapter 1, some part of the accusation material in 2:1—4:4, and the four poems 4:5-8, 13–18, 29–31, and 6:1-8. I would like finally to suggest that that scroll closed with the text of the sermon at the Temple, 7:1-12 (see chap. III). We note that 6:8 says, "Be warned, O Jerusalem"; certainly 7:1-12 is an appropriate closing warning. (If this is the case, then we must assume that later material was subsequently inserted after 6:8, so that 7:1-12 is now separated from what originally preceded it.) In any event, if Jeremiah was preaching words such as those we have examined in chapters 4 and 6, it is hardly surprising that he would be "debarred" or "restricted" from delivering them personally at the Temple (36:5).

The Scroll and Its Scribe

At the beginning of this chapter we pondered the reasons behind Jeremiah's dictating a scroll. He understood the call to dictate it and the necessity of this indirect means of communication. Because Jeremiah was debarred from the Temple, Yahweh took this means of warning the people what would happen if they did not change their ways.

Though it may not be apparent to us today, accustomed as we are to a world filled with printed and written messages, in Jeremiah's day the idea of a prophetic scroll was unprecedented. Jeremiah's was a world of speaking and hearing, not of writing and reading. Only a handful of inscriptions and other written material have come to light in Palestine, in contrast to the libraries of written material from ancient Egypt, Assyria, and Babylon. People committed important material to memory in Jeremiah's day, and memorization was as prized then as it is among Arabs and others in the Middle East today. No earlier prophet wrote down or dictated his material, as far as our evidence goes.[1] The prophets spoke their words and had them committed to memory; and it was only much later that disciples or collectors began to make written material of them.

The one precedent for Jeremiah's scroll is of course the scroll that served as a basis for the reform of King Josiah, the scroll that was evidently the core of the book of Deuteronomy, a scroll that purported to be Moses' words to Israel. So even in producing a scroll, Jeremiah is living out his call to be a prophet like Moses! (see chap. II). And since Jeremiah could not necessarily write, or at least not write easily, he engaged a scribe, Baruch the son of Neriah (36:4, 8).

Of Baruch's career before coming into Jeremiah's life we know nothing. As a scribe, he must have had scribal training; there were surely schools sponsored by the court that trained scribes in the skills of writing and record keeping. He evidently had ready access to other scribes: at a later point in the story he seems on his own initiative to have entered the chamber of the scribe Gemariah (36:10), but he had to be summoned into the presence of the princes at the court (36:14). Perhaps he and Gemariah had been colleagues.

A wonderful archaeological find turned up a few years ago in Jerusalem—a *bulla* of Baruch. An official would carry a stamp-seal, a small seal of stone or gem carved with a design, often with the name of its owner. The seal would be carried either as a ring on the finger or by a cord around the neck. A bulla is a piece of clay impressed with the pattern of a seal. These pieces of clay would be affixed to documents to attest to their validity. The bulla discovered in Jerusalem contains Hebrew letter-forms of the seventh or sixth century B.C.E. with the words "Berechiah son of Neriah the scribe." This is undoubtedly Jeremiah's scribe, so that the biblical "Baruch" turns out to be a shortened form of "Berechiah." With the unearthing of this bulla, we gain a sense of being in touch with the biblical prophet across twenty-six centuries.

There is no direct word about whether Baruch threw in his lot full-time with Jeremiah, but the two men are associated until the very end of the story of Jeremiah (see chaps. VII, X, and XI). And we do have a curious sequence that suggests that Baruch immediately committed himself to share Jeremiah's destiny. He was a modest man and allowed himself in the book of Jeremiah only one small passage from which we learn of his reactions as well, chapter 45, which has only five verses. Since this chapter is dated to the same fourth year of Jehoiakim in which Jeremiah dictated his first scroll to Baruch, it is appropriate to look at it now. Baruch said,

> Woe is me!
>> for the Lord has added sorrow to my pain;
> I am weary with my groaning,
>> and I find no rest.
>
> (45:3)

Clearly Baruch took to heart the terrible words Jeremiah dictated in his scroll. But Yahweh has a word for Baruch, too, a personal word, and it is a word that picks up the four verbs of Jeremiah's call in 1:10 (see chap. II):

> Behold, what I have *built* I am *breaking* down,
> and what I have *planted* I am *plucking* up.

If the verbs "build" and "plant" referred in Jeremiah's call to hope after disaster, then in the word to Baruch they are used of the original hopes and plans of Yahweh for the covenant people, hopes and plans now in danger of being dashed. But beyond the potential disaster, there is this word to Baruch:

> And you, do you seek great things for yourself?
>> Do not seek them;
> For I am going to bring disaster upon all flesh;
>> but I will give you your life as a prize of war
>> in every place to which you may go.
>
> (45:5)

Have no great expectations, please, Baruch, Yahweh says. Be grateful for small favors; in the swirl of persecution and threat of war you can snatch one bit of plunder—your own life. It is all you may expect; do not despise a day of small things (cf. Zech. 4:10).

Now comes the great question: Can the people repent in time?

NOTES

1. The curious wording in Isa. 8:16 hardly counts; the meaning of the text there is uncertain.

RUMORS OF WAR, AND THE ONSET OF A DROUGHT

In chapter V, I described the battles at Carchemish and Hamath in the summer of 605 B.C.E., in which Babylonia suddenly replaced Egypt as the great power in the Near East. I also briefly looked ahead to two events in the following year—the Babylonian destruction of the Philistine city of Ashkelon and the shift of King Jehoiakim from being a vassal of Egypt to being a vassal of Babylon. Now we will review these events and the events of the three years that followed.

The Events of 604 B.C.E.

Nebuchadrezzar had been crowned king of Babylon at the end of the summer of 605 B.C.E. The following year he continued the pressure on the Egyptians: he marched down the coast of Palestine, taking and destroying the Philistine city of Ashkelon (in what is now the Gaza Strip) and deporting the leading citizens to Babylon. Since Ashkelon is only a scant forty miles west of Jerusalem, it came as terrible news to Judah that the army of Babylon was massed to the west!

Jeremiah 47

At this juncture, in the year 604 B.C.E., Jeremiah delivered a poem on the fate of the Philistines, now preserved in chapter 47. It is a curious poem; there is none of the mockery seen earlier in the poem against Egypt in 46:3–12. The first half, vv. 2–3, simply offers a description of the overwhelming flood from the north; the waters, that is, the Euphrates River, symbolize Babylon, rising and overflowing the earth, not stopping for anyone. We do not hear at first of any specific destination for the flood; the language is very vague—"people" (lit. "humanity") "shall cry out" (v. 2). The rumble of horses and chariots so terrorizes everyone that parents do not even stop to grab their children (v. 3). What kind of disaster is this? The reference in v. 4 to Tyre and Sidon (Phoenician cities to the north, in what is now southern Lebanon) is to their potential as allies, so that I would read, "to be cut off by Tyre and Sidon, every surviving helper." There will be no allies to come to the Philistines' rescue. Finally, v. 5 names the specific cities of the Philistines—Gaza and Ashkelon. Verse 6, surprisingly, is a rhetorical address to the sword of the Lord, that it should put itself back in its sheath and be quiet. But this is said in vain, because it is the will of Yahweh that the slaughter continue. Jeremiah thus continues to maintain that the Babylonians' victories were an expression of Yahweh's will.

As noted earlier, the nearness of the Babylonians now forced King Jehoiakim to become a vassal of Nebuchadrezzar (2 Kings 24:1). For his part, Jeremiah evidently continued over the next two or three years to speak out oracles that described the enemy from the north and raised the issue of the status of the covenant people before God.

Jeremiah 5:1–9

One poem that may come from this period is 5:1–9. Yahweh speaks in v. 1 and indicates a willingness still to pardon Jerusalem. However, the ironic condition—that one be able to find within the city someone who does justice and seeks truth—does not bode well for the likelihood of pardon. Indeed the hearers are told to work through the city street by street in the search for that just person: this is reminiscent of the search by the Greek philosopher Diogenes for an honest man! But more to the point, Jeremiah's audience would be reminded of the tradition of Abraham's bargaining with Yahweh over how many just men it would take to spare the city of Sodom (Gen. 18:22–32). At the beginning of that conversation Yahweh told Abraham that he would spare Sodom if fifty just men could be found. Eventually Abraham bargained him down to ten men, but Abraham knew when to quit—ten was as far as he dared go. Does 5:1 suggest that Jerusalem is ten times more wicked than Sodom, if a single just man would save the city?

In vv. 2–6 Jeremiah comments on the situation. Yahweh looks for truth only to hear false oaths. Even when Yahweh inflicts mild punishment on the people, they do not take the hint, refusing to repent (lit. refusing to "turn," vv. 2–3). Then the prophet has an idea: those who refuse to repent are really only the ordinary folk, people without discernment. He, Jeremiah, will go to the leaders of the community. Surely they understand what Yahweh expects of them, for they have had the opportunity to listen to torah. Jeremiah evidently believes that if the leaders set the moral tone for the community, then the rest of the population will follow. But he finds that the leaders too have rejected the discipline of the covenant (vv. 4–5). Therefore, he says, the lion, a metaphor for the Babylonian army, is on its way, joined by the metaphorical wolf and the leopard, lying in wait. Anyone stirring outside the city risks being torn to shreds for their numberless sins and apostasies (v. 6, lit. "turnings," that verb again that we have heard so often).

Yahweh speaks again in vv. 7–9 and continues where he left off at the end of v. 1, almost as if Jeremiah's speech in vv. 2–6 was a negligible interruption. Having given in v. 1 the condition for pardoning the city, Yahweh begins v. 7 with, "How can I pardon you?" The rest of vv. 7–8 depicts the conduct of the people in horrendous fashion: they have abandoned Yahweh in favor of the Baals, who are of course non-gods, and have consequently turned the whole country into one vast whorehouse, the men acting like fancy war-horses neighing for mates (recall the comparison of the people to the female wild ass in 2:23–24). Again, remember that Jeremiah is referring here not only to sexual misconduct but more profoundly to religious harlotry, the idea of everybody frantically craving the security they hoped to find in the Baals.

The conclusion is Yahweh's rhetorical question, "Shall I not punish them for these things, and shall I not bring retribution on a nation such as this?" (v. 9). The impression left by this question is that Yahweh has not yet made a decision but is not far from doing so.

Two other passages, 5:20–29 and 9:2–9, are associated with 5:1–9. Because they close with the same rhetorical question, they are likely to have been uttered during this same period of time. But

before I discuss them, it is necessary that we consider a complicated issue, the date for the great drought that came in those days.

The Great Drought: 601 B.C.E.

At some point in Jeremiah's time there was a great drought.
Jeremiah's description of it in 14:2–6 is vivid and horrifying.
Unfortunately, we have no direct information on which year it
came. There is, however, some indirect evidence that I would like
to discuss now, since it bears directly on the story of Jeremiah.

In chapter V we looked at 36:1–8, the first part of the narrative
of Jeremiah's dictation of a scroll, which took place in 605 B.C.E.,
the fourth year of Jehoiakim (36:1). I did not, however, discuss the
rest of that chapter, though the narrative about the scroll continues, because I believe that there is a gap of four years in the events
narrated. There is reason to believe that the year given in the
Hebrew text of 36:9 (which marks the beginning of the continua-
tion of the narrative), namely, the "fifth" year of Jehoiakim, which
would be of course 604 B.C.E., is a copyist's error, and that the
correct year is the year named in the Greek Septuagint text, the
"eighth" year, which would be 601 B.C.E. This discrepancy of three
years is an important issue in our understanding of the story.

I have several reasons for suggesting the time gap. First, in
Hebrew "fifth" and "eighth" look a good deal alike. One of the
readings is clearly a mistake for the other. It is much more likely
that "eighth" is the *correct* reading and that "fifth" was a conscious
or subconscious "correction" because to a copyist "eighth" would
not immediately "make sense" chronologically after "fourth year"
in v. 1.[1] (Who would change a correct "fifth" to an incorrect
"eighth"?)

A second conclusion can be drawn from the rest of the narrative.
Verse 9 begins the story of the reading of Jeremiah's scroll to the
king at the time a fast was declared, in the ninth month of the
given year (i.e., the end of November or the beginning of December; the ninth month is mentioned in vv. 9 and 22). When the king
hears the contents of the scroll, he burns it (v. 23). What would be
the occasion for a fast at the end of November or beginning of
December? There was no annual fast at that time of year. There
are two strong possibilities.

The first, favored by several commentators, assumes that "fifth year" (604 B.C.E.) is correct; in that event the nation, stunned by the destruction of Ashkelon that very month at the hands of Nebuchadrezzar's army, would have fasted before God. But does it make sense that if King Jehoiakim had declared a fast because of the Babylonian destruction of Ashkelon, he would have burned the scroll that described the very destructiveness of Babylon?

The other possibility, which I accept, is that "eighth year," 601 B.C.E., is correct. At that time, the Babylonian army fought a battle with the Egyptians on Egyptian territory in the Nile Delta, and the Babylonians suffered a serious blow. The perception of King Jehoiakim, then, would have been that Babylon was no longer a threat and he could safely burn Jeremiah's scroll. But in that case, if there was no military emergency, why was there a fast? I suggest that it was because of the onset of the great drought. Note that after the description of the drought in 14:2–6, there is mention of a fast in 14:12.

Perhaps the rains in the winter and spring of 601 B.C.E. had not been generous and the summer had been hotter than normal. Perhaps, too, the normal moist breezes from the northwest were overtaken from time to time by the dry desert wind from the south or east, which the Arabs today call the *khamsin*. When this wind strikes, the humidity plunges. The geographer Denis Baly recalls once, when this desert wind was blowing across Haifa, feeling the shaving cream dry on his face before he could put razor to it.[2] In such conditions pastures wither (Amos 1:2), the wheat crop dries out, and grapes and figs shrivel. Habakkuk 3:17 gives a good notion of what such a drought means; it is even possible that this section of Habakkuk reflects the very drought we are now discussing. If the autumn rains had not come by the end of November or the beginning of December, the declaration of a fast would be a logical decision. Interestingly, there is a much later Jewish tradition, preserved about 200 C.E., that states, "If the first of Chislev [= November/December] was come and no rain had fallen, the court enjoins on the congregation three days of fasting."[3]

From the assumption that the drought occurred in 601 B.C.E., we will now examine Jeremiah's words and actions.

Jeremiah 5:20–29

I have stated that there are two other oracles th.
same rhetorical question—"Shall I not punish t
things?"—found in 5:9: Jer. 5:20–29 and 9:2–9. In 5:
speaks throughout the entire passage, addressing the people as an
exasperated schoolmaster might address refractory pupils: they
are foolish and senseless, using neither their eyes nor their ears
(v. 21). The Hebrew at the beginning of v. 22 emphasizes the
pronouns: "Me do you not fear? Before me do you not tremble?"
As difficult as it is for us to appreciate, the Old Testament notion
is that human fear of God is a good thing; and we cannot water
"fear" down to "reverence"—it really is fear, as the parallel "tremble" indicates. Jeremiah doubtless had in mind proverbial sayings
such as "The fear of the Lord is the beginning of knowledge; fools
despise wisdom and instruction" (Prov. 1:7). Everybody has fears:
why not then choose a life-giving fear, the fear of God? Even the
mighty sea, that old symbol of chaos, has been put in its place by
Yahweh and does not break through the permanent barrier of sand
that is its boundary. The covenant people, however, are constantly
breaking through the boundary of torah that Yahweh has set for
them. Instead of staying with torah, they turn off and go away (vv.
22–23).

Yahweh reminds them in vv. 24–25 that he normally sends the
rain, but that it has been withheld because of the people's sins. It
is altogether possible that the great drought is underway in these
verses.

It may be difficult to understand Jeremiah's explanation of the
onset of the drought as a consequence of the people's sins. On the
face of it, it is hard to accept this linkage. A drought, we assume,
is a result of weather patterns: we watch the meteorological charts
during the weather reports on the local evening news. When
drought is serious there may be church services to pray for rain,
but we are not impelled to confess our sins in order to move God
to send the rain. But Jeremiah took the linkage for granted. To
him, as to earlier prophets, a drought was a signal from Yahweh
that should lead to repentance; think of the drought declared by
Elijah (1 Kings 17:1), and the same message in Amos 4:6–8. The

..ared understanding of Jeremiah and his audience about these matters is important to understand.

Verses 26–28 speak of social injustice. Unfortunately the text of v. 26 is difficult to translate. The NRSV is correct:

> For scoundrels are found among my people;
> they take over the goods of others.
> Like fowlers they set a trap;
> they catch human beings.

That is, when debtors pledge their household goods for debts and then cannot make good on those debts, their creditors take over possession of the household goods in question. The debtors lose their possessions while the creditors greedily pile them up in their houses, collecting them the way a bird-catcher collects birds in a trap. This picture of the terrible contrast between the fat, sleek rich and the helpless poor is broadened in v. 28 to cover the powerlessness of the orphan in court cases (cf. 7:6, discussed in chap. III). What kind of covenant community is this, where the rich take advantage of the poor? And again Yahweh asks the rhetorical question, "Shall I not punish them for these things . . .?" (v. 29).

Jeremiah 9:2–9

That rhetorical question occurs again in 9:9, at the end of the poem in 9:2–9. (It is important to notice that the Hebrew verse numeration is 9:1–8, and some Bibles, including the New American Bible, the New Jerusalem Bible and the New Jewish Version now use the Hebrew verse numbers when they differ from the traditional English ones.)

I have become convinced that Yahweh speaks throughout the entire passage, certainly in v. 3. If Yahweh is speaking in v. 2, it is a startling statement: Yahweh dreams of finding temporary shelter in the desert to take a vacation from the people. Despite the nightmarish nature of the desert (2:6; chap. IV) Yahweh would rather be off in the desert alone, away from all contact with the people, than stay with them any longer. Why? They are all adulterers (cf. 5:7), filled with treachery (cf. 5:27).

Verse 3 specifies what they do. Unfortunately, however, the various translations have not rendered with total accuracy what the Hebrew has:

> They have drawn their tongue, their bow is falsehood, and not for truth are they strong in the land.

The tongue of these people is the arrow (v. 8), shot out by the power of the bow, which is falsehood. "Falsehood" or "the lie" is the motive power that generates their tongues. Why is there this emphasis on the tongue and on false words? Recall the discussion of the power of the word (chap. II). Words are crucial. So how is this "falsehood" or "lie" a motive power? Is it suggestive of Baal, the lie par excellence? So the people proceed from evil to evil; and not only do they not fear Yahweh (cf. 5:22), they do not even know Yahweh (cf. Jeremiah's hope in 5:5).

The third line of v. 4 contains a play on words; in Hebrew the word "supplanter" (*'aqōb ya'qōb*) sounds like "Jacob" (Heb. *ya'aqōb*), who "supplanted" or "deceived" his brother Esau in the old narratives in Genesis, where similar wordplay occurs (Gen. 25:26; 27:36). By vv. 4–6, then, even though Jacob had received the new name "Israel," Israel altogether fulfills the implication of the old name, "Jacob," so that within the community it is neighbor against neighbor, brother against brother, oppression on oppression, deceit on deceit. Within the covenant people, covenant solidarity has melted away.

In v. 7 Yahweh affirms that the people are to be put to a final test: what else can Yahweh do? And the indictment in v. 8 repeats the burden of vv. 3 and 5–6: people use their tongues as deadly weapons. Then, in v. 9, comes the exasperated refrain we have already heard in 5:9 and 29. What else can Yahweh do but punish the people?

Jeremiah 8:4–13

In the fall of 601 B.C.E., the year of the drought, came the next occasion for the reading of the law of Deuteronomy—the feast of booths (the previous occasion was in 608 B.C.E.; see chap. IV). Strikingly, Jer. 8:4–13 implies both the reading of the law and the presence of a drought.

In vv. 4–7 Yahweh raises the question that was raised in 4:1 and implied in 5:3: Why is it so hard for the people to repent? After all (v. 4), when people fall down, one expects them to get up again. Likewise when someone turns off the path, one expects that person to return again.[4] The implication, of course, is that it should be as easy to turn one way as to turn the other. So v. 5 literally reads, "Why then has this people turned in perpetual turning? They hold fast to deceit, they refuse to turn" (this last phrase is the same as the one at the end of 5:3). To Yahweh it makes no sense: in spite of listening carefully, Yahweh has heard no one say he is sorry. Everyone is as headstrong as a war-horse (v. 6; recall the horses in 5:8!). Even the birds keep to their pattern of migration just as, in 5:22, the sea keeps to its assigned place, but Yahweh's covenant people do not know the pattern of conduct assigned to them, that is, the law (v. 7).

Yahweh then turns in v. 8 to address those responsible for the public reading of the law: "How can you say, 'We are wise, and the law of the Lord is with us'?" This rhetorical question implies that those who read the law are not wise at all, just as the similar rhetorical question in 2:23, also prefaced by "How can you say," implied that the covenant people were indeed defiled. The second half of v. 8 offers difficult phrasing; I understand the words to mean, "On the contrary, the lie of the scribes has made the pen into a lie!" That is, the pen, which ought to write the truth, has been turned into an instrument of the lie by the spirit of the scribes themselves. Here again the lie is the motive power for the people, as it was in 9:3. One suspects that Jeremiah hoped his own scroll (likewise prepared with a scribe!) would enjoy a better fate than that suffered by the scroll that had been read to Josiah, the fate of encouraging a complacent spirit, indeed, a lying spirit. Alas, these "wise" leaders will be humiliated and caught: where is their vaunted wisdom? (v. 9); their families and property will be swept away (v. 10a).

(I skip vv. 10b–12; they do not belong here, having been copied here from 6:13–15 in the Hebrew text tradition. They are not found in the Greek Septuagint text at all.)

In v. 13 the three middle lines are evidently a quick, terrible view of the drought—no grapes, no figs, even the leaves on the grapevines and fig trees withered. But the first and last lines of the verse bring difficulties that seem to result from the possibility for multiple meanings. One can read the first line as following directly after v. 10a—God will gather the wives and fields and give them to the enemy. But Jeremiah also intends the line to be heard as a reference to the occasion of the poem, the feast of booths, which is also called "the feast of (in)gathering" (the designation of the feast in Exod. 23:16 and 34:22). But this is a "feast of ingathering" when there are no grapes or figs to gather in. And again the prophet intends "gathering" to suggest an ultimate judgment of the people. The last line of the verse is even more difficult to interpret and seems to be saying several things at once:

1. "what I gave them" (i.e., the law), "they passed over" (i.e., transgressed)
2. "what I gave them" (i.e., the land) "will pass over" (to the enemy), or "will pass away" (i.e., disappear)
3. "what I give them" (i.e., the enemy) "will pass over them" (i.e., overwhelm them)

It is clear from this passage that Jeremiah has become convinced that Yahweh threatens the people with a double punishment: (1) withdrawal of fertility because of their worship of fertility deities, a withdrawal of fertility already underway in the great drought; and then (2) bringing the enemy from the north.

Jeremiah 14:1—15:9

This connection between the drought and the enemy is even clearer in a long passage, 14:1—15:9. The passage clearly encompasses a variety of speakers and audiences. Jeremiah 14:2–6 is a vivid description of the drought; 14:7–9 is a lament of the people in which they confess their sin to Yahweh; 14:10 is Yahweh's summary judgment on the people; 14:11–16 is a dialogue between Yahweh and Jeremiah over the situation (Yahweh speaks in vv. 11–12, Jeremiah in v. 13, and Yahweh again in vv. 14–16); 14:17–18 is a lament of Jeremiah over the people; 14:19–22 is, like vv. 7–9, a lament of the people in which they confess their sin to Yahweh; in 15:1–4 Yahweh addresses Jeremiah and rejects the people's plea; and in 15:5–9 Yahweh offers a mocking condolence over the people, ending with a description of the losses in battle when the enemy comes (15:8–9). This long passage thus begins with a description of the drought (14:2–6) and ends with a description of defeat in battle (15:5–9). In between we hear of "sword, famine and pestilence" (14:12), that is, the double scourge of drought and battle.

What is the character of this passage? A striking parallel in the

Old Testament is the first chapter of the book of Joel. There we hear first a description of the devastation of vines, fig trees, and fields, caused by an infestation of locusts (vv. 4–7, 10), next a call to lamentation and fasting (vv. 13–14), and finally the communal lament (vv. 15–20).

I have proposed that the fast was called in November or December of 601 B.C.E. (36:9, according to the Septuagint text) because of the great drought, an occasion which would undoubtedly have entailed communal lamentation and other liturgy. And 14:12 mentions a fast. What we have then in 14:1—15:9 is Jeremiah's private counterliturgy, the liturgy he understands to be the only valid one to use, as opposed to the liturgy the people did use. In 14:7–9 the people lament, but how grotesque is their notion of Yahweh! They ask, Why should you act like a stranger, a traveler looking around for shelter for the night? Why should you be so confused? Yahweh rejects the pleas of the people (14:11–16), and Jeremiah weeps for the people about to be destroyed (14:17–18). The people try again to manage sincere repentance (14:20), grasping around for any formulation to turn Yahweh's head: "your name's sake," "your glorious throne," "your covenant with us" (14:21). They try very carefully to explain that they really do understand that it is Yahweh who brings rain, not the "false gods of the nations" (14:22). But it is to no avail; Yahweh is through listening (15:1–4).

The passage is heavy with hints of Sheol, the abode of the dead. Thus in 15:5 the Hebrew word for "to ask" (*lish'ōl*) means as well "to Sheol": "Who will turn aside to Sheol about your welfare?" And more than once the term "the land" is a euphemism for Sheol. Thus, 14:18 implies, "Both prophet and priest ply their trade in the *Land* where there is no knowledge," that is, the land of the dead. In 15:7 God has "winnowed them in the gates of the *Land*," the gates of the underworld. It is a horrifying scene, surely a far cry from whatever hopeful words the people used in their public liturgy.

In Jeremiah's perception, death is already looming over the people.

What will happen to this troublesome prophet and his dark words? The narrative of 36:9–32 will tell the story.

NOTES

1. Other commentators assume "fifth" is correct. See, e.g., Wilhelm Rudolph, *Jeremia* (Tübingen: J.C.B. Mohr, 1968), 230. For the suggestion that "eighth" is correct, see Norbert Lohfink, "Die Gattung der 'Historischen Kurzgeschichte' in den letzten Jahren von Juda und in der Zeit des babylonischen Exils," *Zeitschrift für die Alttestamentliche Wissenschaft* 90 (1978), 324–28.

2. Cf. Denis Baly, *The Geography of the Bible*, rev. ed. (New York: Harper & Row, 1974), 52.

3. The reference is found in the Mishna, *Taanith* 1:5. See Herbert Danby, *The Mishnah* (Oxford: Oxford University Press, 1933), 195.

4. The Hebrew is wonderfully trimmed down. The second question in v. 4 is simply, "If one turns, does he not turn?" leaving the audience, which has heard the opposing verbs of the previous question, to hear these two verbs as opposites as well.

VII | THE KING BURNS THE SCROLL, AND GOD SETS THE PLAN IN MOTION

In late November or early December of 601 B.C.E., the very time when the fast was declared in Jerusalem, the Babylonian army was in trouble in the Nile Delta in Egypt (see chap. VI). Babylon was constantly searching for the way definitively to defeat Egypt and perhaps was hoping to extend its control down into Egypt proper, as Assyria had done seventy years before. So the two armies joined battle in the Nile Delta, and if the Babylonian army was not defeated, it is clear that both sides suffered heavily and that Nebuchadrezzar led his troops back to Babylon to regroup. Word of the blow to Babylon must not have been long in coming to King Jehoiakim: it was now clear to him that Babylon could be defeated! Then and there he threw off his vassalage to Babylon (2 Kings 24:1).

Baruch Reads the Scroll:
Jeremiah 36:9–31

The date of the public fast, by my proposal, was the end of November or the beginning of December in 601 B.C.E., called because of the continued drought. For Jeremiah it is another opportunity for people to hear God's words proclaimed, but since he is barred from going to the Temple area personally, he sends his scribe Baruch to the Temple precincts to read the scroll he had dictated four years before (36:9). Baruch goes first to the chamber of a fellow scribe, Gemariah (36:10). Though Gemariah himself is evidently not present, his son Micaiah is, among others, and Baruch reads them the contents of the scroll (cf. v. 13).

When Micaiah hears the contents of the scroll, he is alarmed enough to go off to the secretary's chamber at the palace to report the matter. There several officials are sitting, some of whom are named. It is interesting to speculate how the various officials might have reacted to the news of the scroll. Gemariah himself, the father of Micaiah, might have been sympathetic: Gemariah's brother Ahikam had protected Jeremiah when he was in danger after the occasion of the Temple Sermon eight years before (26:24; see chap. III). On the other hand, Elnathan son of Achbor was the official who led the posse that King Jehoiakim had sent to Egypt to arrest Uriah the prophet at that same period of time (26:22; see again chap. III); he is not likely to have been so sympathetic.

In v. 14 the officials send one of the scribes, Jehudi (cf. vv. 21, 23), to call Baruch in to read the scroll to the officials, and he does so (v. 15). The wording of v. 16 is harsh, literally, "They trembled, each to the other." The officials feel obliged to tell the king, not to get Jeremiah and Baruch into trouble (v. 19 suggests some at least were trying to protect them) but because the matter of the validity of the words of the scroll is urgent. The question the officials ask Baruch in v. 17 is curious: "How did you write all these words?" as is his naive answer in v. 18: "with pen and ink." The officials are asking whether the scroll is really what it claims to be, that is, the result of Jeremiah's dictation. On the other hand, Baruch, sensing the direction of the questioning, does not volunteer any information about the way he has become involved with Jeremiah, choosing instead to answer in the most noncommittal way possible. He prefers not to get involved any more than he needs to; after all, he is simply following Jeremiah's orders. The officials keep possession of the scroll, but they tell Baruch—and Jeremiah—to go into hiding (v. 19).

The officials deposit the scroll in an adjoining room and report the whole matter to King Jehoiakim (v. 20). The king immediately sends the scribe Jehudi to fetch the scroll, while he himself keeps warm by a stove (vv. 21–22). We are reminded by this of the month (cf. v. 9), a month when it can be cold in Jerusalem. Jehudi reads the scroll to the king and the other officials, but the king gives Jehudi orders to burn the scroll, section by section (it is Jehudi, not the king, who wields the scribe's knife in v. 23; so rightly the NJV).

And so it is done. The words of the scroll have no effect on those who hear it: no one tears his garments in dismay (v. 24)!

The narrative of this chapter contains parallels with the narrative of chapter 26, the consequences of Jeremiah's Temple Sermon. But it is clear that parallels are also intended with the story of the discovery of that earlier scroll of Deuteronomy narrated in 2 Kings 22—23 (cf. chap. II). As the scribe Shaphan was the central figure in bringing the scroll of Deuteronomy to King Josiah (2 Kings 22:3, 8–14), Shaphan's son Gemariah is a central figure in bringing Jeremiah's scroll to King Jehoiakim (Jer. 36:10, 12, 25). And if, while when King Josiah heard the scroll of Deuteronomy, he tore his clothes (2 Kings 22:11), when King Jehoiakim hears Jeremiah's scroll, no one tears his clothes (36:24). Instead, the scroll itself is torn and burned.

Various readings in the Greek Septuagint suggest that something has been dropped from the present text of 36:25; I would reconstruct it as follows:

> Elnathan and Gedaliah had also urged the king to burn the scroll, but Delaiah and Gemariah urged him not to burn the scroll.

Thus, two advisors urged him to destroy the scroll (cf. my remarks on Elnathan above) and two advisors urged him not to.

But, one might ask, why would Jehoiakim want to burn the scroll at all? Why not simply arrest Jeremiah? According to v. 29, the king had asked, "Why have you written, 'The king of Babylon will indeed come in and destroy this land and remove from it man and beast'?" Certainly the king must have been unfriendly toward Jeremiah for years, since word of Jeremiah's utterances such as 22:13–19 would certainly have reached his ears (see chap. III). If the king had any suspicion that Jeremiah was a true prophet, by burning the scroll he could help rid the land of the effect of the prophet's words. On the other hand, if the king had the suspicion that Jeremiah was a false prophet—and, after all, the scroll must have been heavy with words about the foe from the north, whereas Babylon had just suffered a setback at the frontier of Egypt—his words were nonsense and should not be allowed to survive. In any case the king is a man of action, and he orders the arrest of Baruch and Jeremiah. In this, however, he is not successful; they remain hidden.

At this point (vv. 27–32) Jeremiah experiences a fresh revelation from Yahweh, a revelation that represents a major shift in his understanding of his calling. Yahweh pronounces punishment on the king: the king will have no successors, and when he dies his dead body will not be buried (recall the earlier pronouncement on the king's death, 22:18–19). The king, his offspring, and his officials will be punished for their iniquity. But, more than that, the whole people will suffer the disaster that Yahweh had planned against them, because they cannot respond (v. 31).

Here is the shift! Until now, the purpose of the scroll had been to warn (vv. 3, 7; see chap. V). But the king does not respond to the warning: he burns the scroll. How can the people respond if the king, who represents the people, does not respond? We recall Jeremiah's move from the ordinary people to the leaders of the people in 5:4–5. The king's burning of the scroll is the catalyst for the shift in Jeremiah's perception: no longer are the scenarios of the enemy from the north simply scenarios, plans, or possibilities in Yahweh's hands; now Yahweh will irrevocably set the plan in motion.

The Second Scroll: Jeremiah 36:32

Now, of course, for Jeremiah the words recorded on the scroll have not been lost; he has all his material in his head. He simply tells Baruch to prepare another scroll, and into this second scroll he dictates not only the contents of the old scroll but much else besides (v. 32). This new material will include not only oracles that have come to Jeremiah's mind since the battle of Carchemish in 605 B.C.E. but fresh, doom-laden material that stresses the irrevocability of God's plan of destruction for the people. To this material we now turn.

Jeremiah 4:9–12, 19–28

When I examined 4:5–31 in chapter V, I skipped vv. 9–12 and 19–28; it is time now to look at these two passages. They need to be looked at together because they both seem to have been delivered during the same period of time. Certainly they share a striking sequence of four key words. The first two of these key words are "heart," which occurs twice, and then "soul," terms that often parallel each other in the Old Testament (e.g., "You shall love the Lord your God with all your heart and with all your soul"). In 4:9 "heart" appears twice in the Hebrew text: the New Jerusalem Bible translates:

> That day, Yahweh declares, the king's heart will fail him, the princes' hearts will fail them too.

Then the Hebrew word I refer to as "soul" *(nephesh)*: it covers a great array of meanings—"self," "life," "breath," "throat." This word appears in v. 10, "The sword is at the throat." The other two key words are not parallels but share the *same sounds* in Hebrew— "desert" *(midbār)* and "speak" *(dabbēr)*. Thus in v. 11 we see "desert," and in v. 12 we see "speak."

This same sequence of words appears in vv. 19–28. Thus at the beginning of v. 19 we see "heart" twice. And at the end of v. 19, though the translations do not reflect it, Jeremiah addresses his own soul rhetorically: "For you hear the sound of the trumpet, O my soul, the alarm of war" (see the alternative reading at this spot in the NRSV). Then in v. 26 we see "desert," and in v. 28 the verb "speak" ("I have spoken"). This identical sequence of four key words suggests that vv. 9–12 and 19–28 are intended to balance each other and to be heard together.

Now it is noteworthy that in v. 28 Yahweh has decided irrevocably to destroy:

> For this the earth shall mourn,
>   and the heavens above be black;
> for I have spoken, I have purposed;
>   I have not relented nor will I turn back,

or, as the Greek Septuagint translates the last four phrases,

> I have spoken, and I have not relented;
> I have purposed, and I will not turn back.

(Verse 27 seems to be a mitigation, and I deal with that verse below.) My proposal then is that when Jeremiah dictated his second scroll to Baruch, he not only redictated 4:5–8, 13–18, and 29–31, poems from four years before (the time of the Battle of Carchemish), but inserted *between* them these two new poems, vv. 9–12 and 19–28, that reflect God's irrevocable decision to destroy the people. Let us examine them now in detail.

Verses 9–10 are easy to read, but much stands behind the words. Verse 9 reads,

> In that day, says the Lord, courage shall fail the king and the officials; the priests shall be appalled and the prophets astounded.

That day will be the day of defeat in battle, and on that day both the king and his officials in the palace and the priests and prophets at the Temple will be demoralized, paralyzed, unable to function. Then v. 10,

> Then I said, Ah, Lord God, how utterly you have deceived this people and Jerusalem, saying, "It shall be well with you," even while the sword is at the throat!

We have met the phrase "Ah, Lord God" before, in Jeremiah's call (1:6; see chap. II). The phrase communicates Jeremiah's dismay. Here his dismay is that Yahweh seems deliberately to be deceiving the people. How would Jeremiah come to this conclusion?

Jeremiah understands Yahweh to have said to the people, "It shall be well with you," or, as the NJB has it, "You will have peace." How would Yahweh have said a thing like that to the people? The answer is through optimistic prophets. It will help to look once more at 14:13, part of the drought and battle liturgy we examined in chap. VI. In that verse, which begins with the same expression of dismay, "Ah, Lord God," we read, "Here are the prophets saying to them, 'You shall not see the sword, nor shall you have famine, but I will give you true peace in this place.' " These optimistic prophets must have been associated with the Temple, and they must have been wonderfully reassuring to the king and the court and the people. Jeremiah's first thought (4:10) is that these prophets are legitimate, true prophets, sent by Yahweh, it is true, but sent by Yahweh to deceive people—for what reason Jeremiah cannot fathom. But if the optimistic prophets are the true prophets, what becomes of Jeremiah's call: is he a false prophet? Yahweh reassures Jeremiah with another explanation:

> The Lord said to me, "The prophets are prophesying lies in my name; I did not send them, nor did I commend them or speak to them. They are prophesying to you a lying vision, worthless divination, and the deceit of their own minds." (14:14)

Yahweh reassures Jeremiah that Yahweh is not deceiving the people and that Jeremiah is a true prophet. The optimistic prophets are fooling themselves; whether they know it or not, their words are worthless. I return to the problem of the optimistic prophets, and Jeremiah's relation to them, in chap. VIII.

Jeremiah 4:11–12 reinforces the word of doom. Though the Hebrew text of these two verses offers several difficulties, it is clear that it describes the hot wind from the desert, which, as I noted earlier, would have contributed to the drought (see chap. VI).

In 4:19–22 is an interchange between Jeremiah and Yahweh: Jeremiah speaks in vv. 19–21, and Yahweh in v. 22. In his speech Jeremiah is frantic with emotion; the NJB translates v. 19 as:

> In the pit of my stomach how great my agony! Walls of my heart! My heart is throbbing! I cannot keep quiet, for I have heard the trumpet call, the battle cry.

The words translated "in the pit of my stomach" are literally "my bowels, my bowels." Jeremiah is overcome by emotion as he envisages the battle to come, the battle that will mean the destruction of his people. In v. 20 he continues to describe his vision: " 'Crash after crash' is the cry" (my trans.); the people now shout in panic that building after building has collapsed. How long, Jeremiah asks, do I have to continue to endure such a vision? (v. 21).

But if Jeremiah spoke with high emotion of "my bowels, my bowels" (Heb. *mē'ay mē'ay*, v. 19), Yahweh turns the consonants around and talks with cold calm of "my people" (Heb. *'ammî*, v. 22), as if to say, You may be concerned about your bowels, Jeremiah, but I am concerned about my people. Yahweh speaks as a schoolmaster giving the same grade to failed pupils in six successive lines: My people are foolish, me they do not know, they are stupid children, they have no understanding, they are skilled in doing evil, but how to do good they do not know." They get A's in wickedness and F's in goodness!

There follows in vv. 23–26 one of the starkest poems in the Bible. In it Jeremiah envisages not only the destruction of his people but the destruction of all creation.

> I looked to the earth, to see a formless void,
> and to the heavens, and their light was no more;

> I looked to the mountains, to see them quaking,
>   and all the hills rocked to and fro;
> I looked, to see no one at all,
>   and all the birds of the heavens had fled.
> I looked, to see the fruitful land a desert,
>   and all its cities laid in ruins,
>   before the Lord, before his fierce anger.
>
>   (4:23–26, my trans.)

The poem is very carefully put together, like a delicate piece of jewelry. Four times the verses begin with "I looked." Looked at what? At four visions of non-life (earth, heavens, mountains, hills), and at four visions of life (human beings, birds, fruitful land, cities). The images are nicely balanced: human beings live on the earth, birds in the heavens. The images of v. 23 carry us back to Genesis 1: "formless void" is the same Hebrew phrase translated as "without form and void" in Gen. 1:2; and of course "their light was no more" is the negation of Gen. 1:3. At the same time the image of v. 25, "I looked, to see no one at all" (lit. "I looked, to see no man") carries us back to Gen. 2:5 ("and there was no man to till the ground"). The imagery of v. 26 is that of the Israelites entering into Palestine: "fruitful land" is the same Hebrew word as "plentiful land" in Jer. 2:7, and "desert" of course was mentioned in 2:6. Thus, the poem moves from the concern with creation in vv. 23 and 25 to the concern with the covenant people and Palestine in v. 26.

At first glance the order of images in this poem strikes us as anticlimactic. We might feel a little more comfortable if the terms were reversed, that is, if we began with Palestine and human beings and birds and ended with heaven and earth. But recall, from the discussion of 2:6 (chap. IV), that in the Old Testament one begins not with creation but with redemption, with the liberation of the exodus. Here in Jer. 4:23–26 redemption is the climax, the ultimate purpose of God's efforts. The ultimate concern of God is the quality of life maintained by the community. If that is gone, if the rescued people have forgotten their rescuer, then all of creation may disappear as well. Jeremiah envisages a time of chaos and dark night, when confusion reigns as it reigned before God's great wind began to brood over the face of the waters (Gen. 1:2).

Yahweh's speech (vv. 27–28) appears to reinforce Jeremiah's vision; certainly v. 28 does, as we have already seen. I propose that the consonantal text of the Hebrew of v. 27 originally had a different set of vowels, so that the verse would have read,

> For thus said the Lord, "The whole earth shall be a desolation, and none of it will I remake."

If that is the case, then Jeremiah's sense of Yahweh's intention for the world is utterly bleak.

Jeremiah 5:10–17

Jeremiah 5:10–17 is another passage that reflects this message of Yahweh's irrevocable decision to destroy. The vine in v. 10 is a metaphor for Israel (cf. 2:21; see chap. IV); and the vine is to be destroyed. The second line evidently originally said, "and make a full end"; commentators surmise that the "not" was a later addition to the text.[1] Israel, the vine, is a people who are intended to belong to the Lord (2:3) but who do not, as a matter of fact (5:10). Jeremiah speaks to Yahweh (v. 12), complaining of the optimistic prophets; Yahweh speaks to Jeremiah (v. 13), stating that the prophets, who claim to speak in the spirit (Hebrew *rūaḥ*), will become wind (another meaning of the Hebrew *rūaḥ*). And in the last line of v. 13 I propose this reading: "scorching shall come to them."[2] This line is then followed by the image of fire in v. 14.

But there is in v. 14, I suggest, one more necessary shift: the last part of v. 14 ("I am now making my words in your mouth a fire, and this people wood, and the fire shall devour them") must be read as the first part of v. 14—for it is the close of Yahweh's word to Jeremiah. Then begins Yahweh's speech to the people, the first part of v. 14. That is to say, I suggest that vv. 13–14 originally read as follows.

> (Yahweh addresses Jeremiah:) But the prophet shall become wind, and the word is not in them, scorching it shall become to them! I am going to make my words in your mouth into fire, and this people into sticks, and it will eat them (vv. 13, 14b).
> (Jeremiah speaks to the people:) Therefore thus Yahweh God of hosts has said (v. 14a).

And this is followed by Yahweh's speech, vv. 15–17. Because the people have been invincibly contrary to Yahweh, Yahweh is putting into the mouth of Jeremiah, Yahweh's prophet, words that will burn up the people. These words, specifically, are the words describing the people from the north, awesome people who will come in and bark orders in a language the people of Jerusalem cannot possibly understand (v. 15) and who will eat and eat and eat, flocks and vines and fig trees (v. 17) that, as a matter of fact, have not been growing so well lately (8:13; 14:2–6).

Jeremiah 8:14—9:1

A similar poem is found in 8:14—9:1. This passage, too, can be read without much difficulty, though a few remarks are useful. The wording of v. 14 is based on the wording of 4:5 (see chap. V): the people speak, agreeing to run to the safety of the walled cities, but they know it is useless, that they will die there. Yahweh speaks in vv. 16–17, describing as usual the disaster to come. Jeremiah expresses his sad dismay at the people's behavior (v. 18) and quotes the people's fatuous questions: Is not Yahweh at the Temple? Is it not business as usual? These questions are interrupted by Yahweh's exasperated counterquestion, "Why have they provoked me to anger with their graven images, and with their foreign idols?" (v. 19). This leaves the people limply observing, It's awfully late in the summer, and we're not saved yet (v. 20). Jeremiah then gives voice to his own dismay over the shattering of his people (8:21–22; 9:1).

Jeremiah 9:17–22

But perhaps the most striking poem from this period is 9:17–22. Here the professional funeral women are addressed and given the words to the lamentations they are to practice for the coming funeral of the city of Jerusalem. It happens that the feminine plural verbs are long, elaborate forms of the verb and take a long time to pronounce. Imagine the stiff old women told to hurry, hurry, all in slow time. Then, vv. 21–22 ("Death has come up into our windows . . .") offer the content of the lament. There was a god of death in Canaanite mythology, and it is likely that Jeremiah has the old myth in mind: Death itself creeps all the way into the central citadels of the city to cut off young and old: corpses will drop and stay unburied, like dung out on the fields.

There are more poems of the same sort in 6:9–15, 16–21, and 22–26; they are easily read and understood with knowledge of the themes Jeremiah proclaimed in this period. In 6:27–30 we have another, final, report card on the people similar to that in 4:22, but this time Jeremiah administers the examination on behalf of Yahweh and comes up with a similar verdict of failure: "Refuse silver they are called, for the Lord has rejected them."

Jeremiah the Anti-Moses

If Jeremiah's very words are to burn the people (5:14), it is no wonder he is shattered by both the task and the prospect. Worse, the prophet, who is always expected to pray for his people (cf. Amos 7:1–6), is now forbidden by Yahweh any longer to pray for them: both 7:16–20 and 14:11 state this categorically. Jeremiah, once the prophet like Moses (chap. IV), is now an anti-Moses figure, since Moses was the great intercessor (see 15:1, where the two intercessors Moses and Samuel are mentioned). Indeed, if Jeremiah tries to pray for the people, Yahweh simply will not hear him (7:16). The people are busy baking cakes for the "queen of heaven" (7:18), Astarte, the fertility goddess (see the discussion of Baal and Astarte in chap. IV). And 7:20 emphasizes the motif of "burning" once more. Did the fact that King Jehoiakim burned Jeremiah's scroll stimulate this emphasis on the burning of the land?

All of this raises a basic question. Granted that Jeremiah understands the necessity for Yahweh to punish those who have disobeyed (5:9), but surely Jeremiah can see the unfairness of a divine punishment that is so all-encompassing as to destroy babes in arms, children, and innocent old folks, along with the guilty. The rhetoric of 6:11 is terrible. What kind of God can Jeremiah understand, who would undertake such a gross and undifferentiated destruction?

The first thing to be said is that this was an old problem for Israel. It was part of the conversation between Abraham and Yahweh in Gen. 18:23 over the proposed destruction of Sodom: "Will you indeed destroy the righteous with the wicked?" a story Jeremiah surely knew (cf. the discussion on 5:1 in chap. VI).

Second, Jeremiah's own emotional reaction to the coming destruction of the people (4:19–21; 8:18, 21–22; 9:1) is doubtless based on this issue. In the course of these poems one sees the phrase "my poor people" (lit. "daughter of my people," 4:11; 6:26; 8:19, 22; 9:1), a personification of the people as vulnerable and pathetic. Jeremiah does not enjoy what he is convinced he has to do, a matter we shall explore further in chapter VIII.

But, it must be said, the Old Testament understands the covenant people as a total community; they will sink or swim as one.

Yahweh's Command to Abstain
from Marriage

There is one more step in Jeremiah's life to be explored now—his obedience to Yahweh's calls for celibacy and isolation. That is the meaning of 16:1–9.

These are fresh calls to Jeremiah. Verses 1–4 command him not to marry and to have no children, as a sign to the people that Yahweh has decreed the end. People are going to die in the land, they shall not receive proper burial, and the vultures and dogs shall feed on their corpses. Perhaps this sign is to be seen as a development of Hosea's sign to the people over a century before: Hosea was called to marry a prostitute, as a sign that the people's relation to Yahweh was corrupt (Hosea 1:2). Now Jeremiah is to marry no one at all, as a sign that the covenant relation is null and void.

It is clear that the undertaking of this sign, the sure sign of the irrevocability of the people's doom, is conceivable only after the king has burned the scroll. If Jeremiah was born in 627 B.C.E., he would at this point be twenty-six or twenty-seven years old. This consideration, it must be said, is another argument for understanding 627 B.C.E. to be the year of Jeremiah's birth; if he had begun to preach in 627 B.C.E., then by 601 B.C.E. he would have been roughly forty years old, an unlikely age to declare his abstention from marriage (see chap. II) or to be considering marriage.

Further, Jeremiah is called not to attend funerals and weddings (16:5–9). In a village society, weddings and funerals are the great times, the high times, the memorable times, the times of great emotion. Nothing else matters so much as that these events go properly. A bride will save for years for a wedding dress (cf. 2:32);

pity, then, the orphan girl who has no family to help her with her wedding preparations! And regarding funerals, imagine not allowing the professional funeral women to do their work (cf. 9:17–22). What games do children play? The only games worth playing, really—weddings and funerals. This, we must understand, is the presupposition of Jesus' little parable in Matt. 11:16–17. And from all this Jeremiah was to abstain. Imagine the scandal this abstention would have caused.

The abstention from marriage, however, was an even greater scandal. There is no parallel for such a call in the rest of the Old Testament; no one else undertook such a gesture. We in our time are accustomed to the existence of celibate priests and to lay men and women who abstain from marriage, but there was no such notion in Israel.

Moreover, so far as we can tell, there was no clear notion of a life after death among the Israelites. Yahweh was a God of the living, not of the dead, and people understood themselves to live on in their children. Notice, for example, how God's address to Jacob in Gen. 28:14 mixes a personal address with a prediction of his children; the verbs are singular in Hebrew: "you [singular] shall spread abroad to the west and to the east and to the north and to the south." Jacob *is* his children; Jacob gains a new name, Israel (Gen. 32:28); Jacob is the *nation* Israel. The head of the family *is* his family and lives on in it. So for Jeremiah to be deprived of the opportunity for children is for Jeremiah to become extinct. No more awesome sign could be imagined. In the eyes of his fellow citizens this must have seemed a monstrous sentence. What it meant, of course, was that Jeremiah felt himself forced to depend entirely upon Yahweh; Yahweh was his sole support.

And soon Jeremiah would raise questions about Yahweh; we shall explore how this came about in the next chapter. But for now we are left to ponder the personal cost God may exact from those who would be faithful.

NOTES

1. J. Philip Hyatt, "Exegesis of Jeremiah," in *The Interpreter's Bible* (Nashville: Abingdon Press, 1956), 5:847, states that "not" is probably a mitigating gloss. See my *Jeremiah 1*, Hermeneia (Philadelphia: Fortress Press, 1986), 183, for a discussion of the matter.

2. For a justification for this reading, see again my *Jeremiah 1*, 183.

VIII PRIESTS AND PROPHETS AGAINST JEREMIAH, AND JEREMIAH AGAINST GOD

Antagonizing the Temple Authorities and Prophets

We saw in the last chapter that when King Jehoiakim burned Jeremiah's scroll, the prophet and his scribe went into hiding to avoid arrest by the king. But not only the king was after Jeremiah.

Jeremiah 19:1–20

At some point during this period, at a time when he was not in hiding, Jeremiah offered a public symbolic action of God's irrevocable punishment, as a consequence of which he was locked in the stocks overnight. The translation "stocks" is only a guess; we do not know exactly what kind of device for confinement was used. The incident is recounted in 19:1—20:6. No date is given, but it is clear that Jeremiah makes a public declaration of the coming disaster on the people, so it is appropriate to examine it here.

Jeremiah understands Yahweh to command him to buy a pottery flask and then to take several elders of the people and senior priests with him to the Potsherd Gate in Jerusalem. This "flask" was a water-jar with handles, a wide belly, and a narrow neck; its name in Hebrew, *baqbuq*, imitates the gurgling sound water makes as it is poured. One wonders how sympathetic or unsympathetic these men were to Jeremiah's message, but of course there is no way to know. The location of the Potsherd Gate is not known either: it is associated with the Valley of Hinnom (19:2) on the east side of the Temple Mount and was doubtless a gate through which trash was thrown out of the city into the valley.

Jeremiah is told what to say on this occasion. The key word is "make void" (19:7; Hebrew, *baqqōtî*, a pun on the flask, *baqbuq*). Yahweh is going to *make void* the plans of Judah and Jerusalem. Jeremiah is to break the flask (19:10) in front of his witnesses and say, "Thus says the Lord of hosts: So will I break this people and this city, as one breaks a potter's vessel, so that it can never be mended."

The senior priests who had been witnesses to Jeremiah's smashing the flask were doubtless those who passed the word to Pashhur, the priest in charge of keeping order in the Temple area (20:1). Jeremiah was arrested, and Pashhur beat him and put him in the stocks overnight (20:2). Pashhur released him the next morning, but the night hours had given the prophet a chance to brood on what Pashhur had done to him. And so, in the morning Jeremiah greeted Pashhur with a word from Yahweh, a word that involves a shift of Pashhur's name (20:3). Some wordplay is evidently involved, though it is not altogether clear what the wordplay is. I have suggested that Jeremiah twisted Pashhur's name (*pashhūr*) into the Aramaic *pāsh-sehōr*, which means "fertile on every side," and then stated that God announced a new name for him, the opposite, "terror on every side." He goes on to offer a scenario of disasters that the new name portends for the priest (20:4–6).

This word, coming through Jeremiah, that Yahweh intended to rename Pashhur, would not have endeared Jeremiah to the Temple authorities.

Jeremiah 23:9–33

But the optimistic prophets were evidently the chief source of enmity toward Jeremiah. Jeremiah became understandably exercised about these prophets at this period; we have already seen his dismay over their optimistic words in 14:13–16 and 4:10. Jeremiah 23:9–33 is a long sequence on these prophets (vv. 34–40 are in a different style, and commentators suggest that they were added by someone else a century or more later).[1] Though this sequence may not be a single utterance but several related ones, all of it seems to stem from this period. Notice that the drought is still underway (v. 10) and that the prophets have an optimistic message (v. 17), as they do in 14:13–18.

The indictment that Jeremiah levels at the prophets in Yahweh's name is devastating. Jeremiah himself is reeling with emotion (v. 9; cf. 4:19). How can the priests and the prophets in the Temple ("in my house," v. 11) take hope from the Babylonians' setback in Egypt? There can be nothing but bad news ahead (v. 12). Though the prophets in the northern capital, Samaria, had turned to Baalism (v. 13), the prophets in Jerusalem are worse, and are making the city as bad as Sodom and Gomorrah (v. 14). The prophets are the source of sacrilege ("ungodliness," v. 15).

Yahweh instructs the people not to listen to these prophets (vv. 16–17). The optimistic prophets have not stood in the presence of Yahweh; if they had, they would have proclaimed Yahweh's true words and brought about the repentance of the people (vv. 18, 21–22). Now there is nothing but bad news ahead—the tempest of Yahweh (v. 19). You will see it soon enough (v. 20). Yahweh is not a kind of buddy, under our control, but rather the awesome God who made heaven and earth (vv. 23–24). Yahweh may be near (can we hear the confident words of the optimistic prophets, that God is near to them?) but is far off as well. The prophets may claim true revelation, but all they do is borrow each other's words, trivialities as unsustaining as straw, while Yahweh's true words are like fire or a smashing hammer (vv. 25–32).

Now in v. 33 comes one more twist of the knife. A technical term in Jerusalem for a prophetic oracle was a "burden" (e.g., in Isa. 13:1, the KJV has "burden," the RSV has "oracle"). Here, Yahweh tells Jeremiah that if anyone asks him what the "burden" is, he is to answer, "You are the 'burden'!"

These utterances earned Jeremiah the enmity of the optimistic prophets not only because they obviously resented such a negative judgment, but for a very particular reason. Deuteronomy 18:20 states that a false prophet must die. The question then at any time is, Given two prophets who offer opposite words, who is the true prophet and who the false? It was of course not clear early in the year 600 B.C.E. whether good news or bad news would rule the day. But for the optimistic prophets, Jeremiah was a thorn in the flesh, and if good news is the word from Yahweh, then the purveyor of bad news must be done away with.

The Confessions of Jeremiah

This is the background of one of the most remarkable collections of passages in the Old Testament, the so-called confessions of Jeremiah. This term is not very adequate, but it is the term to which scholars have become accustomed. Jeremiah's "confessions" are really complaints or laments to Yahweh, for some of which answers from Yahweh are recorded. As I indicated in chapter I, there are no passages comparable to these in the rest of prophetic literature (one may think of Jonah, but Jonah offers a kind of farcical opposition to God, not the kind of soul-shaking struggle Jeremiah offers). It is possible that other prophets were impelled from time to time to complain to God, but there is no trace of such complaints in the books called by their names.

My own analysis suggests that the confessions of Jeremiah were shaped at two points in his career—now, that is, perhaps early in the year 600 B.C.E., and then six or seven years later, in the summer of 594 B.C.E. Since I am working chronologically, I shall discuss the first set here and the second set in chapter IX. These passages reveal Jeremiah's own spirit both in his trust and in his doubt. Unfortunately there are many difficulties working against understanding the confessions themselves.

Jeremiah 11:18–23

The first confession is 11:18–20; Yahweh's answer to it comes in vv. 21–23. The first line of v. 18 comes on suddenly: I propose to read it as the Septuagint does and understand the first line as Jeremiah's self-quotation; " 'O Yahweh, inform me so I can know it!'—that was when you showed me what they are doing." By this reading we know that Jeremiah has at some earlier point gotten wind of a plot against him and has prayed to Yahweh that Yahweh give him the details. Jeremiah now affirms that Yahweh has granted the request and has shown Jeremiah what his enemies are planning. Jeremiah reiterates in v. 19 that he has been unaware of the plot, as innocent as a lamb being led to slaughter. The verse then offers a quotation from the plotters. The first line of the quotation does not really say, "Let us destroy the tree with its fruit"; the Hebrew text seems to say, "Let us destroy the tree in its bread," an expression that makes no sense. I suggest a slight variation, "Let us destroy the tree by his opponent."[2] If this is the correct understanding of the line, then Jeremiah's enemies are devising a way to get at him, though of course there is no way now to identify the "opponent"—somebody like Pashhur, perhaps. His enemies want to chop him down like a tree. The quotation of the enemies continues, "Let us cut him off from the land of the living, that his name be remembered no more." It is ironic that they should say this, given the fact that Yahweh has already called Jeremiah not to marry and have children (chap. VII). By Yahweh's command, Jeremiah is already cut off from the land of the living, and his name will be remembered no more. (I return to this at the end of chap. XI.)

In the face of these appeals of his enemies, Jeremiah turns to Yahweh in prayer (v. 20). He addresses Yahweh as the "righteous judge," but we may also understand him to be addressing Yahweh as "the judge of the innocent man." Jeremiah understands himself to be the innocent party in this dispute, and he wants Yahweh to judge in his favor. The second line is, literally, "who assays the kidneys and the heart." The kidneys are the inmost organs, and in the Old Testament they are the seat of the inmost sentiments. The heart is seat of the character, the decision making. Yahweh knows men and women through and through. The third line of v. 20 is better translated as "Let me see your retribution upon them" (NRSV) than "Let me see thy vengeance upon them" (RSV); the noun in question—retribution—has to do with the exercise of legitimate governmental authority. Jeremiah is innocent, he is convinced, and he needs to have the injustice he has suffered rectified—this is what he is asking of Yahweh.

Verses 21–23 bring Yahweh's answer. I suggest that v. 21 is a later expansion by Jeremiah (see chap. IX), as is the phrase "upon the men of Anathoth" in v. 23. By this understanding the answer has nothing to do with the men of Anathoth but rather with Jeremiah's current enemies, the optimistic prophets (see below). Yahweh's answer is intended to reassure Jeremiah; Yahweh says, in effect: I will indeed destroy them, because they will die when disaster comes upon the whole nation, when their young men and their children shall die by sword and famine. The bad news you are announcing is the correct news. Note here the same pairing of "sword" and "famine" that we found in Yahweh's word against the optimistic prophets in 14:13–16 (see chap. VI), and note the similarity between the last part of 11:23 here and the last part of 23:12 in the sequence on the false prophets, which we looked at earlier in this chapter. This similarity helps establish that it is indeed the optimistic prophets who are plotting against Jeremiah at this point.

Jeremiah 12:1–6

In 12:1–6 Jeremiah's lament to God is in vv. 1–4 and Yahweh's answer in vv. 5–6. The first three lines of v. 1 need some careful work.

The RSV translation of the first line is in a way correct: "Righteous art thou, O Lord." However, the Hebrew word translated "righteous" also means "innocent," and since the next two lines use the language of the lawcourt, it is clear that Jeremiah begins his speech to Yahweh with the words "Innocent are you, O Lord" ("You will be in the right, O Lord," NRSV).

The second line in the RSV is also fuzzy. The phrasing is the same as in 2:9, where God levies an accusation against the people, or indicts them. Here Jeremiah says, "when I indict you" ("when I lay charges against you," NRSV). Jeremiah is speaking in bitter sarcasm to Yahweh: "You will be innocent, O Lord, when I indict you." But the third line is the clincher; it does not say, as the RSV has it, "yet I would plead my case before thee." Rather, it reads, "yet I would pass judgment upon you." A good parallel is 39:5, where the same phrase appears: there Nebuchadrezzar passes judgment and sentence upon King Zedekiah.

What Jeremiah says to Yahweh, in effect, is, All these years I have been your messenger to your people, while you have sued them for breach of contract. But now, O Lord, you have broken your promise to me: you promised you would be with me to deliver me (1:8). So now I want to take you to court to sue you for breach of contract. Oh, I know, if I do, you will find a way to be innocent, but I will have my day in court with you even so. The New Jewish Version (NJV) catches it best: "You will win, O Lord, if I make claim against You, Yet I shall present charges against

You." This sentiment is picked up in the book of Job when Job confesses his inability to get fair treatment in his quarrel with God (Job 9:13–20).

And what, specifically, is Jeremiah's charge against Yahweh? That comes in the second half of v. 1 and the first half of v. 2:

Why does the way of the guilty prosper?
   Why do all who are treacherous thrive?
You plant them, and they take root;
   they grow and bring forth fruit.

Jeremiah is contrasting his situation with the one so confidently portrayed in Psalm 1. There innocent people are like trees planted by streams of water that yield fruit in their season, while guilty people are like chaff that the wind blows away. But Jeremiah's experience is to the contrary: it is the guilty who are like trees planted by streams of water that yield fruit in their season. Why? Why? The guilty claim Yahweh to be near with their words, but Yahweh is far from their hearts (that is, from their character). These guilty are evidently still the optimistic prophets, who, we have seen, confidently claim Yahweh to be near (23:23).

In v. 3 Jeremiah assumes that Yahweh knows Jeremiah's innocence; he therefore prays that Yahweh will treat his enemies as sheep destined for slaughter rather than allow him to be a lamb led to slaughter (11:19). And in v. 4 Jeremiah affirms that the drought is still upon the people, a drought, he is convinced, that is Yahweh's response to a wicked, heedless people.

Yahweh's response comes in v. 5 (I take v. 6 to be a later addition, just as was the reference to the "men of Anathoth" in 11:21 and 23; see chap. IX, p. 111). If Yahweh's response to Jeremiah in 11:22–23—that punishment really was coming—was to be heard as reassuring, Yahweh's response to Jeremiah in 12:5 is alarming: Jeremiah, if you think it is bad now for you, it is going to get worse.

If you have competed with foot-runners and they have wearied you,
   how will you compete with horses?

There may be an innuendo to the verb translated here as "compete" or "run" that escapes us; in 23:21 Yahweh says, "I did not send the [false] prophets, yet they ran." "Running" therefore represents the activity of the prophets, and as Jeremiah tries to "race" with them, he has grown discouraged. But worse is to come—the time when he will have to race with horses (Babylonian horses? the rigors of battle?). The implication of Yahweh's answer is that Yahweh knows exactly what he is doing and is very much in control of what is happening to Jeremiah.

Jeremiah 15:15–19

There is another complaint of Jeremiah's from this period in 15:15–18, and an answer from Yahweh in 15:19. I take vv. 20–21 to have been added at a later point (see chap. IX). In v. 15, as he did in 11:20, Jeremiah again asks Yahweh's retribution on Jeremiah's persecutors. Though Yahweh is well known for being slow to anger and abounding in steadfast love (Exod. 34:6), Jeremiah ironically asks that Yahweh not be so slow to anger as to neglect Jeremiah's persecutors altogether.

We looked at v. 16 in chapter II, in terms of the chronology of Jeremiah's life. I suggested that (1) "your words were found" is a reference to finding the Deuteronomic scroll in the Temple in 622 B.C.E.; and (2) "and I ate them" is Jeremiah's subsequent acceptance of his call. He goes on in this verse to affirm that his acceptance of the call had about it at first some of the joys of a honeymoon: he is called by Yahweh's name as a bride is called by her husband's name.

Then in v. 17 Jeremiah affirms that he has been a loner, not sitting "in the company of merrymakers"—an ironic reference to the optimistic prophets—but bearing isolation because of his prophetic vocation, "under the weight of your hand" to proclaim Yahweh's wrath, "for you had filled me with indignation."

The result, for Jeremiah, has been only endless pain and a lack of response from Yahweh:

> Truly you are to me like a deceitful brook, like waters that fail.
>
> (v. 18)

This is appalling to Jeremiah. He had been a spokesman for Yahweh, proclaiming Yahweh to the people as the spring of running water which they had abandoned only to replace with leaky cisterns (2:13; see chap. II). But though Jeremiah had proclaimed

Yahweh to be the spring that never runs dry, when all is said and done Yahweh ironically has become for Jeremiah "a deceptive stream with uncertain waters" (NJB). What hope is there for the prophet? If Yahweh is the sole support of the prophet (see chap. VII), and that support fades away, then what hope is there? Jeremiah is suffering a kind of dark night of the soul.

Yahweh's answer in v. 19 is again surprising. He says, in effect: Jeremiah, you have been preaching repentance to the people, now try repentance yourself.

> If you turn back, I will take you back,
>   and you shall stand before me;
> if you utter what is precious and not what is worthless,
>   you shall serve as my mouth.

If you repent and speak sound words instead of garbage, then you can still be my prophet. "It is they who will turn to you, not you who will turn to them": the people need you, you do not need the people. Though one person with God may be a majority, it is a terrible life to live out.

Jeremiah 17:5–8

But in spite of the lack of any sign of Yahweh's presence in his life, Jeremiah is willing to reaffirm his faith in Yahweh. This I take as the meaning of 17:5–8. These four verses, like 12:1–2, are a variation on Psalm 1. But in contrast to 12:1–2, this time Jeremiah has the good folks and bad folks sorted out right.

> Cursed are those who trust in mere mortals
>   and make mere flesh their strength,
>   whose hearts turn away from the Lord.
> They shall be like a shrub in the desert,
>   and shall not see when relief comes.
> They shall live in the parched places of the wilderness,
>   in an uninhabited salt land. (vv. 5–6)

By contrast,

> Blessed are those who trust in the Lord,
> . . . .
> They shall be like a tree planted by water,
>   sending out its roots by the stream.

It shall not fear when heat comes,
  and its leaves shall stay green;
in the year of drought it is not anxious,
  and it does not cease to bear fruit. (vv. 7–8)

The people who trust in mere mortals are like a shrub in the desert, while people who trust in the Lord are like a tree planted by water. Yes, as does Psalm 1, Jeremiah has the good and bad people sorted correctly. But there is still a difference from Psalm 1, because in Jeremiah's words those who trust in God are like trees planted by water that continue to give forth leaves and fruit *even in a year of drought*. The drought on the land is still very much on Jeremiah's mind, but it is the spiritual drought—Yahweh the deceitful brook, Yahweh the waters that fail—that really concerns him, and he presses ahead to affirm his faith in that God for whom he can discern no evidence at all.

Jeremiah 18:18–23

There is one more "confession" that belongs in this period, 18:18–23. In v. 18 we hear the words of the plotters, and in vv. 19–23 Jeremiah's words to Yahweh. In contrast to the time when the prophet expressed to Yahweh his horror that the punishment on the people was coming (4:19–21), now he prays that it come, so that his standing as a true prophet might be validated (vv. 21, 22a). The psychic cost of such a prayer must have been overwhelming. Yahweh has made a decision to punish the people, but when, oh when, will it be clear? And it is striking that there is no answer from Yahweh here.

These prayers, or confessions, are astonishing in their honesty and in their freedom. Even more astonishing is the fact that they were preserved as part of the story of Jeremiah. Why they should have been preserved is something of a puzzle; I shall return to the question in chapter IX. For now we must simply marvel that the community of believers held on to these words in which Jeremiah shakes his fist at Yahweh as part of their tradition of Yahweh's dealings with them.

Jerusalem Besieged: 599–598 B.C.E.

We must now pursue the historical events of the next two years. As noted earlier, in December of 601 B.C.E. the Babylonian army suffered a setback at the hands of the Egyptians in the Nile Delta, following which King Jehoiakim threw off his vassalage to Nebuchadrezzar. Nebuchadrezzar did not for the moment have the means to punish Jehoiakim for his rebellion. Instead he contented himself, probably in the course of 599 B.C.E., with sending client tribes or raiding parties against Judah from across the Jordan, Ammonites and others (see 2 Kings 24:2).

But Jeremiah continued to be convinced that Babylon would strike, and in December of 598, the Babylonian army marched against Jerusalem and besieged it. In that same month King Jehoiakim died. It is possible, since he was the one responsible for the nation's predicament, that he was assassinated. His son Jehoiachin, just eighteen years old, was put on the throne (2 Kings 24:8).

Jeremiah 10:17–25

It is in these circumstances, I suspect, that Jeremiah delivered the oracle found in 10:17–25. The city is addressed as a refugee woman:

Gather up your bundle from the ground,
  O you who live under siege! (v. 17)

Yahweh will "sling out" all the inhabitants of the land into exile (v. 18). The people lament in vv. 19 and 20; and Jeremiah remarks in v. 21 that the "shepherds" (the rulers, cf. 2:8) are stupid, so their flock is scattered. Then in v. 22 Yahweh reiterates the announcement of the great "commotion" or earthquake from the north, the Babylonians, that will leave the cities of Judah desolate.

The oracle ends in a surprising way in vv. 23–25. The people speak, but they are quoting Scripture. Verse 23 is a variation of Prov. 16:9, which says, "A man's mind plans his way, but the Lord directs his steps." The people piously quote that proverb here to avoid taking blame for their predicament. Yahweh may have told the people to "stand at the crossroads, and look, and ask for the ancient paths, where the good way lies, and walk in it" (6:16, see chap. VII), but the people insist that it is not in their power to direct their own steps: "I know, O Lord, that the way of human beings is not in their control, that mortals as they walk cannot direct their steps."

Verse 24 is a variation of Psalm 6:1, which says, "O Lord, rebuke me not in your anger, nor chasten me in your wrath." Here the people say, "Correct me, O Lord, but in just measure; not in your anger, or you will bring me to nothing." That is, a tap on the wrist is all right, God, but nothing heavier or you will wipe us out. Then where will your promise to Abraham be—to make us as many as the stars of the heavens or the sand of the sea (Gen. 22:17)?

Verse 25 cites Psalm 79:6–7, in which Yahweh is asked to pour out wrath on the nations that do not know Yahweh because those nations have devoured Jacob (i.e., Israel and Judah). So, a tap on the wrist will do for the covenant people, but if Yahweh is really set on being wrathful, pour that wrath out on other nations, not us.

For a long time Jeremiah had offered Scripture to the people as guidance (4:1–4), Scripture from Hosea and Deuteronomy (see chap. IV). Here, in contrast, is the Scripture the people prefer to cite. No wonder Yahweh is bringing the Babylonians to besiege the city of Jerusalem!

Jeremiah 22:24–27, 28–30

The young King Jehoiachin was quick to surrender to Babylon. Babylonian records give the date as March 16, 597 B.C.E. Two short passages, 22:24–27 and 22:28–30, deal with Jehoiachin at the time of the surrender ("Coniah" is another form of "Jehoiachin").

In 22:24–27, Yahweh says he is going to "hurl" the king and the queen mother into a foreign land from which they will never return. The verb reminds us of the word in 10:18, that Yahweh would "sling" out the inhabitants of the land.

The second passage, 22:28–30, is more poignant. Why is Jehoiachin like a broken pot, cast aside? Why are he and his children hurled off to an unknown land? Verse 29 says starkly: "O land, land, land, hear the word of the Lord," something Judah could never do.

And v. 30, "Write this man down as childless," reads as if it is instructions being given to the officer of prisoners of war, to record

Jehoiachin as just one more refugee. "Childless" is not to be taken literally but as meaning "without an heir on the throne."

Jehoiachin, his wives and children, the queen mother, other members of the court, and several thousand others were taken into captivity along with much treasure (2 Kings 24:12–16, but cf. Jer. 52:28). Jehoiachin lived on for many years in Babylon: after thirty-seven years in exile, he was released from prison by Nebuchadrezzar's successor (2 Kings 25:27), who supported him and gave him a certain status in exile (2 Kings 25:28–30).

On the throne in Jerusalem Nebuchadrezzar put another member of the royal family, Zedekiah, who was a brother of Jehoiakim and thus an uncle of Jehoiachin. The result of course was a division of loyalty among the people over who was the legitimate king— Jehoiachin, a prisoner of the Babylonians in exile, or Zedekiah, whom the Babylonians had placed on the throne?

For some reason, Jeremiah was not among those exiled. It may be that he stayed outside the city during the siege or that, if he was within the city, he was marginal to the circles of power whom the Babylonians chose for deportation. The priest Ezekiel, however, was among those exiled and after five years in Babylon would himself hear a call to prophesy (Ezek. 1:1–3). It is possible that Ezekiel had been acquainted with Jeremiah before the siege of Jerusalem.

But if many were deported to Babylon, many also were allowed to stay in Jerusalem. And the question must have come particularly to the minds of those who remained in Jerusalem: If God was to punish us, is this it? We have lost so much of the treasure of the Temple, our youthful king, and so many of our leaders, but even so, we are still here. We have survived. There is still a king of the line of David on the throne. We can live to fight another day.

We must see how Jeremiah dealt with these issues.

NOTES

1. See William McKane, *Jeremiah,* International Critical Commentary (Edinburgh: T. & T. Clark, 1986), 1:602–4; and my *Jeremiah 1,* Hermeneia (Philadelphia: Fortress Press, 1986), 647–48.

2. Giving a different set of vowels, reading *belōḥamô* instead of *belaḥmô.* This word "opponent" occurs in Ps. 35:1 (RSV and NRSV, "those who fight against me").

PRAY FOR THE PEACE
OF BABYLON

After Jerusalem's surrender to Babylon and the appointment of
Zedekiah as king, two questions lingered in people's minds. The
first was, Who is the legitimate king, Jehoiachin in exile, or Zedekiah, put on the throne as a puppet of Babylon? Jeremiah was
evidently in no doubt, for in 23:5–6 he offered a word that some
day a legitimate king would come whose name would be not
"Zedekiah" but, turning the king's name around, "Yahweh-zid-
kenu" (i.e., "Yahweh is our righteousness"). That is, even though
the name "Zedekiah" might mean "Yahweh is righteousness,"
Zedekiah is not Yahweh's legitimate king. On the other hand,
Jeremiah was no enthusiast for Jehoiachin; Jeremiah believed the
boy king would be lost to history.

The second and inevitable question in the minds of those who
were allowed to stay in Jerusalem after the siege of 597 B.C.E., was,
Is this all there is to God's punishment? And inevitably another
thought crept in: Those who were deported to Babylon have been
punished, but we were not. They must have been guilty while we
were not. It was the fault of our leaders, and it is they who are
suffering, not we.

Complacency: Jeremiah 24

More complacency! and Jeremiah reacted. In chapter 24 we have
an account of a vision he had in this period, perhaps a vivid
dream, a vision of two baskets of figs offered on the altar in the
Temple—a basket of prime ripe figs and a basket of putrid figs.
The prime ripe figs, Yahweh explains, represent the exiles in
Babylon, whom Yahweh will some day bring back home and who

will be the nucleus of the covenant people. The putrid figs, on the other hand, represent King Zedekiah, his court, and the people who remain in Jerusalem, whom Yahweh will make an object of contempt, and against whom Yahweh will send sword, famine, and pestilence until they are destroyed. The exiles in Babylon represent the real continuity between past and future, the folk whom Yahweh has sent out into the unknown in a faraway land will return for a new start with a new heart, and in that new start the covenant will be secure. Those who have stayed at home, who carry on the normal activities of life in Jerusalem, represent a dead end, and they can only expect more catastrophe in time to come.

Babylonian Idolatry:
Jeremiah 10:1–16

Since Jeremiah was convinced that continuity lay with those in exile, he made every effort to keep in touch with them. I propose that 10:1–16 is a message he sent to the exiles. (Though there are scholars who believe the passage, which sounds similar to passages in Isaiah 40—55, was not uttered by Jeremiah, I accept it as genuine to him.) It begins, "Do not learn the way of the nations . . . for the customs of the peoples are false" (vv. 2–3).

The poem swings back and forth from a mockery of idols (vv. 2–5, 8–9, 14–15) to hymnic lines proclaiming the God of Israel (vv. 6–7, 10, 12–13, 16). The climax of the poem, v. 11, is a witty saying about the false gods, offered in the Aramaic language, which had by then become the common language in Babylon.

Idolatry made sense to those who worshiped the various gods and goddesses of the nations. Because people repeated myths about their gods and goddesses, it was natural for them to construct some visual representation of their deities. And since Marduk was the high god of Babylon (he is mentioned, with the spelling "Merodach," in 50:2), his temple would house a great image of him, in precisely the same way as the palace housed the king. People would see in the image of a deity the embodiment of the deity. And just as the king in the palace was clothed and fed by his attendants, so in the temple the idol was clothed and fed by the priests. During the New Year's festival, the idol was carried around the city so that the deity could assert his authority over the realm for the coming year.

Jews, of course, were well aware of the Ten Commandments, one of which forbade them to make any image for worship. Moses had taught the people to attend to the *hearing* of the *words* of God, words that move and are dynamic, rather than to depict God in a static way. So when the exiles arrived in Babylon, they must have been both horrified and fascinated by the images they saw, huge images glittering with silver and gold, richly clothed in purple (10:9). Here, dazzling their eyes, were what they had always been forbidden to have anything to do with, right out in the open for everyone to see. Furthermore the exiles must have heard from their Babylonian captors, over and over again, remarks such as, Marduk won the war for us. Who is that God you say you worship?—Yahweh? Well, obviously Marduk is stronger than Yahweh. There he is, over there; have a good look at him.

Hence Jeremiah warned the Jews in exile, "Do not learn the way of the nations, . . . for the customs of the peoples are false" (10:2, 3). And he mocked the system of idolatry at its weakest point: *People* make *idols* (vv. 3–4, 9), whereas the true God made the earth (vv. 12–13). Idols just stand there lifeless (vv. 4–5), whereas the true God is the living God (v. 10). Idols do not speak (v. 5), whereas when the true God speaks, there is a tumult of waters in the heavens (v. 13). There is no reason to be afraid of idols (v. 5), even when there are portents in the heavens (v. 2), because idols cannot do anything at all, either evil or good (v. 5). By contrast, at God's wrath the whole earth quakes (v. 10). Indeed, idols are nothing more than scarecrows in a cucumber field (v. 5), whereas the real God formed all things. Furthermore, of all things, Israel is the tribe of God's inheritance (v. 16)!

The climax to this series of contrasts is v. 11, in Aramaic. Jeremiah must have known Aramaic: we saw his pun on Pashhur's name (20:1–6), a pun that evidently involves Aramaic (see chap. VIII). There is no way to put this two-line poem into smooth enough English to show what is going on, but literally it reads,

> The gods who the heavens and the earth did not make, let them
> perish from the earth and from under the heavens, these.

Two things must be said. First, when the poem was recited, there would have been a bit of uncertainty as to whether the first word meant "the gods" or "God," an uncertainty cleared up only at the end of the first line of the poem, where the verb "did not make" has a plural form. Second, the words "make" and "perish" sound identical in Aramaic. The poem makes it clear that the idols not only did not *make* the heavens but are not even *in* the heavens. They are *under* the heavens, and the last word, "these," emphasizes the foolish plurality of these gods. And Jeremiah said all this in the language of Babylon, so that the Babylonians and their idols could receive the message directly.

The Events of 594 B.C.E. and Jeremiah's Reaction

We now turn to the cluster of events in Jeremiah's career that took place in 594 B.C.E. The prelude to these events took place in Babylon in December 595, or January 594 B.C.E. At that time there was an attempted uprising against Nebuchadrezzar by some of the Babylonian military units. Nebuchadrezzar got word of it and put it down brutally: he boasted that he executed the ringleader with his own hands. But in the next few months a report of the attempt must have gotten back to Jerusalem, raising the hope that if the little states there in the west could combine forces, they might be able to throw off the domination of Nebuchadrezzar. There may also have been hope for help from Egypt because a new pharaoh, Psammetichus II, had just come on the throne.

Jeremiah 27

Accordingly, sometime in the late spring or early summer of 594 B.C.E., King Zedekiah called ambassadors from Edom, Moab, Ammon, Tyre, and Sidon to a "summit conference" in Jerusalem (Jeremiah 27). To Jeremiah, this was all foolishness: he was convinced that for the moment Yahweh had given Nebuchadrezzar dominion over not only Judah but the whole world, and over not only human beings but animals as well (vv. 5–6). In acting out his conviction he followed a divine command to make a necklace of thongs and yoke-pegs (v. 2). Palestinian yokes of the time consisted of a beam that lay across the shoulders of the oxen, with pairs of pegs jutting down from the beam that fitted on either side of the neck of each ox and were tied by thongs under the neck.

Jeremiah made a necklace of thongs and yoke-pegs to demonstrate that he, at least, was ready for Nebuchadrezzar's yoke. Then Jeremiah walked in on the summit conference to give identical necklaces to each of the ambassadors, telling them to "send them" (i.e., the necklaces, v. 3, NEB and NJB) to their kings, preparing them, too, for the yoke of Nebuchadrezzar.

With the gift for each king came a message to take back (vv. 5–11). This message is striking, one of the few instances in the Old Testament of a message about Yahweh's will preached by someone from the covenant community to an audience of foreigners. In this situation, of course, Jeremiah does not speak of Yahweh's covenant with Israel but rather of Yahweh's dominion over creation. He tells them that since Yahweh has given that dominion over to Nebuchadrezzar, a dominion extending even to the animals in the field, then the kings should not listen to any of their prophets or soothsayers who tell them they are not going to have to submit to the king of Babylon (vv. 9–10). So any hope the kings might have to rebel against Nebuchadrezzar is in vain. Jeremiah has a similar word for the host, King Zedekiah: any prophets who tell you that you do not have to submit are lying. Submit! (vv. 12–15).

Jeremiah 28

There is no record of how the king and the ambassadors responded to Jeremiah's interruption of their conference. We do, however, have a narrative of Jeremiah's encounter with one of the optimistic prophets in the Temple area, at just this period, in chapter 28. The prophet was Hananiah, and the encounter took place in the "fifth month" of that year, July or August of 594 B.C.E. Hananiah was evidently quite sincere, and he offered a word that he proclaimed had come from Yahweh, "I have broken the yoke of the king of Babylon; within two years I will bring back from Babylon all the vessels from the Temple, and king Jehoiachin and the other exiles" (vv. 2–4).

Jeremiah's response is bemused: Amen! May the Lord do so; may he perform your words and return the vessels and the exiles. Nevertheless, the prophets that preceded you and me from ancient times prophesied war; so when the word of a prophet who prophesies peace comes true, then we will know that the Lord really sent that prophet (vv. 6–9). Good news is easy, so it is better to be cautious; it is bad news that fits the pattern of prophetic words of the past.

Jeremiah is still wearing his necklace of thongs and yoke-pegs, so Hananiah goes up to him and breaks it, announcing, "This is how I will break the yoke of the king of Babylon within two years." Jeremiah's symbolic action is bested by Hananiah's symbolic action. And all Jeremiah can do is "go his way" (vv. 10–11). Who is the true prophet, the purveyor of good news or the purveyor of bad news?

Jeremiah evidently prays about this question, because a fresh word from Yahweh comes to him, a word for Hananiah: "You may have broken the wooden yoke-pegs, but they will be replaced by iron ones: because God has placed on all the nations not a wooden yoke of Nebuchadrezzar's but an iron yoke" (vv. 12–14). And the close of Jeremiah's word to Hananiah is to involve a play on words, after which he raises the ante: "Listen, Hananiah, the Lord did not *send* you to prophesy. You have had people trust in a lie. But the Lord says, Look, I will *send* you off the face of the earth. This year you shall die" (vv. 15–16). If Hananiah prophesies that the yoke of Nebuchadrezzar will be lifted within two years, Jeremiah prophesies that Hananiah will die within one year. The narrator adds laconically that two months later Hananiah did die (v. 17). I shall return to the matter of Hananiah's death later, when I discuss the reading of the law of Deuteronomy in 594 B.C.E.

Jeremiah's Letter to the Exiles:
Jeremiah 29:1–23

Meanwhile, Jeremiah had sent a letter to the exiles in Babylon to try to dampen their enthusiasm for the possibility of an early release from captivity (29:1–23). The letter is more than a letter from Jeremiah to the exiles, however; it is also a word from Yahweh: the last phrase in v. 23—"I am witness, says the Lord"—means "I countersign." "Witness" was the standard term of the day for someone who countersigned a letter or other document.

If it is odd for a letter to be countersigned by God, the letter begins with another oddity. All letters of the period began with a salutation that had some expression for "peace": "peace to you," or "peace to you and your family," or the like (cf. Paul's letters in the New Testament, e.g., Rom. 1:7). But this letter has no salutation; v. 5 simply plunges into the body of the letter, giving the reader the sense that the writer is rude and abrupt. Where is the polite salutation, the greeting of peace? It is deferred; first are the instructions to the exiles to build houses, plant gardens, marry, have children, plan marriages for your children, settle down in Babylon (vv. 5–6). Then in v. 7 comes the deferred word about peace:

> Seek the welfare [*shalom*, "peace"] of the city where I have sent you into exile, and pray to the Lord on its behalf, for in its welfare [peace] you will find your welfare [peace].

In other words, you are looking for the normal greeting of peace? You have work to do; and when you get your work done, you will hear the word of peace.

And what is this work? It is to abandon the outlook of prisoners of war. Prisoners "do time"; they count the days until their release, days that are essentially empty. They are tempted to jump at every rumor that says release is coming. No; to the contrary, settle down because the action is in Babylon. You are not there accidentally, victims of bad luck. I have sent you there deliberately, and you will be there a long time (cf. the paraphrase in 29:28). Do not live your days moping for Jerusalem. Live your lives there, in Babylon, and live them fully. For now put aside the prayer of Psalm 122:6, "Pray for the peace of Jerusalem!" Learn a new prayer, "Pray for the peace of Babylon!" for in Babylon's peace you will find your peace.

This is, of course, an astonishing word: how can we pray for our captors? This letter from Jeremiah was probably less attractive to the exiles than were the words of the poet among them who composed Psalm 137:

> How shall we sing the Lord's song in a foreign land? If I forget you, O Jerusalem, let my right hand wither . . . O daughter of Babylon . . . happy shall he be who requites you with what you have done to us!

Shemaiah's Letter about Jeremiah:
Jeremiah 29:24–32

Jeremiah's letter caused a prophet among the exiles named Shemaiah to write a scathing letter to Zephaniah, one of the priests in Jerusalem. Zephaniah was responsible for law and order in the Temple area, just as Pashhur had been earlier (see chap. VIII). Shemaiah asks the priest why he has not arrested Jeremiah for writing such a letter to the exiles (29:24–28) and implies that Jeremiah is a "madman" (v. 26). Zephaniah shows Shemaiah's letter to Jeremiah, and Jeremiah simply responds with a word from Yahweh: Shemaiah is a false prophet, and Yahweh will punish him (vv. 29–32).

A Prophet Further Besieged:
More Confessions of Jeremiah

When Hananiah had broken the yoke-pegs off Jeremiah's neck (28:11), it could not have been entirely clear to Jeremiah who the true prophet was and who the false. After all, Hananiah had won the day. And it is now, I propose, six or seven years after the earlier confessions, that Jeremiah renews his confessions to Yahweh, using not only those previous confessions (see chap. VIII) but fresh ones as well.

Jeremiah 11:21, 23; 12:6

It is at this time, too, I suggest, that Jeremiah incurred opposition from another quarter—his village and, in particular, his family. When, in chapter VIII, we examined the confession in 11:18–23, I skipped both v. 21 and the phrase "men of Anathoth" in v. 23. It is now, I suggest, that these words come into Jeremiah's perception of Yahweh's answer: As to the men of Anathoth, the people of Jeremiah's village, Yahweh will punish them, along with everyone else. And in discussing Yahweh's answer in 12:5–6, I skipped v. 6. Here, again, I suggest that it is at this time that v. 6 became part of Yahweh's answer: It is not only the men of your village who are after you. Even your brothers, even your father's clan, even they have betrayed you: this is the word from Yahweh to the prophet. But things are worse, as the next line in v. 6 indicates. The Hebrew says, "They have cried, 'Full!' after you." I suggest that "Full!" here means "Drunk!"[1] The prophet Shemaiah in Babylon implied that Jeremiah was a madman; now the members of Jeremiah's family seem to be accusing him of being a drunkard.

Why would his family have persecuted him? There could of

course be any number of reasons. The very fact that Jeremiah had challenged the authorities in Jerusalem could well have made him an embarrassment to proud village people. The optimistic prophet Hananiah was from Gibeon, just west of Anathoth (28:1); perhaps Jeremiah's family wondered why Jeremiah was not like Hananiah. Another possibility is related to Yahweh's call to Jeremiah to abstain not only from marriage but even from attending weddings and funerals, as a sign of the end (see chap. VII). That abstention might well have been the last straw for his family; perhaps Jeremiah stayed away from the wedding of a cousin as a religious act. How can that be? his family would have felt. It is a scandal, bringing nothing but shame on everyone. Jeremiah's words, "Under the weight of your hand I sat alone" (15:17), take on new meaning as his family rises against him.

Jeremiah 15:10–12

I turn now to a passage of confessions that appears to be from this period, 15:10–12. Unfortunately, these verses offer several problems in interpretation. Jeremiah speaks in v. 10. Is this poetic address to his mother a reflection of persecution by his brothers and his father's clan (12:6)?

> Woe is me, my mother, that you ever bore me, a man of strife and contention to the whole land! I have not lent, nor have I borrowed, yet all of them curse me. (NRSV)

Yahweh answers in vv. 11–12:

> I swear I have armored you well, I swear I have intervened with you in a time of disaster and in a time of distress. (v. 11, my trans.)

Yahweh will ultimately make sure that Jeremiah is protected in his difficulties. Then v. 12:

> Can he break iron, iron from the north, and bronze?

I suggest that (1) "he" refers to Hananiah, and (2) this response came to Jeremiah after Hananiah broke the wooden yoke-pegs from Jeremiah's neck and Yahweh told him that the wooden pegs would be replaced with pegs of iron (28:10–13). Can Hananiah break iron yoke-pegs? Can Hananiah break iron from the north—

the iron yoke of Babylon? As a matter of fact, since Jeremiah evidently perceives that Yahweh is making him a fortified wall of bronze (1:17–19; 15:20–21), can Hananiah break the bronze into which I am making you? In spite of all his doubts and difficulties, then, Jeremiah hears a word of reassurance from Yahweh.

Jeremiah 17:14–18

Yet Jeremiah continues to be poised between faith and doubt. I suggest that the confession in 17:14–18 comes from this period; in it the prophet once more pours out his dismay and prays to Yahweh for healing. And it is noteworthy that to this lament there is no recorded answer from Yahweh.

Jeremiah 20:7–12; 11:1–13; 20:13

In 20:7–12 Jeremiah turns in bitterness against Yahweh. The verb in the first line of v. 7 *(pittah)* means not only "deceived" (RSV) but also "seduced" (NJB). It is used of a man "seducing" a virgin in Exod. 22:16. The NRSV covers both meanings with "enticed."

Convinced as he has been that he is a true prophet, how can Jeremiah now accuse God of having deceived him? Worse, Jeremiah, who has thought God's relationship with him was similar to a marriage (15:16; see p. 98), now accuses Yahweh of seducing him, overpowering him, and then tossing him aside—and Jeremiah has allowed himself to be seduced. He has preached nothing but bad news, and that bad news has brought him nothing but contempt and derision (v. 8). If he comes to his senses and simply decides not to speak out anymore, "Then within me there is something like a burning fire shut up in my bones; I am weary with holding it in, and I cannot" (v. 9). The imagery is much like that in Yahweh's words of destruction in 5:14 and 6:11, which we noted at the end of chapter VII.

Who were the "many" who are whispering, "Terror on every side" (v. 10)? Clearly, it is those who opposed Jeremiah. Jeremiah's opponents in 11:18–19, I suggested, were the optimistic prophets (see chap. VIII), and they were doubtless among the "many" here, but Jeremiah also included in this group all his familiar friends. Jeremiah continues to feel deeply isolated. We recall that "Terror on every side" was Jeremiah's new name for Pashhur (see p. 92);

one can imagine bystanders saying, "Here comes old 'Terror-on-every-side' again!" His opponents look for a chance to entice him and overpower him (v. 10), when ironically, by Jeremiah's accusation, Yahweh has done just that already.

All Jeremiah can do in the face of this is to resort to his rock-bottom faith in Yahweh, who will fight on his behalf, and to affirm that ultimately he himself will be vindicated. He even prays once more the prayer he had prayed six years before (v. 12; cf. 11:20; see p. 95).

Jeremiah 11:1–13

Before discussing 20:13, some background is necessary. Late September or early October in 594 B.C.E. was once more the occasion for a public reading of the law of Deuteronomy (cf. the public reading in 601 B.C.E. in connection with 8:4–13 in chap. VI). I suggest that Jeremiah delivered 11:1–13 on the occasion of the reading in 594. The passage contains overtones of Deuteronomy, notably the reference to "this covenant" (vv. 3, 8), and the phrase "so be it" (lit. "amen") in v. 5, which seems to mimic the "amens" in Deut. 27:15–26.

There are some characteristics of the passage that suggest this particular year. First is the reference in v. 4 to "the iron furnace" as a description of Egypt—Jeremiah clearly had "iron" on his mind during this period. And there is the remarkable statement in v. 9 that "conspiracy exists among the people of Judah and the inhabitants of Jerusalem." The word "conspiracy" occurs nowhere else in the book of Jeremiah, but it is an apt description of King Zedekiah's attempt to draw the neighboring kings into revolt against Nebuchadrezzar. According to Jeremiah, however, a conspiracy against Nebuchadrezzar is a conspiracy against Yahweh, since Yahweh is Nebuchadrezzar's sponsor; the people "have broken my covenant which I made with their fathers" (11:10). Jeremiah continued then, in spite of the temptation to stop expressed in 20:9, to speak out the bad news that Yahweh gave him to speak.

Something else happened during that festival: the prophet Hananiah died. Jeremiah 28:17 declares that he died in that same year, in the seventh month. The seventh month is the month for the festival of booths, during which Deuteronomy was to be read.

Given the confrontation between Hananiah and Jeremiah in the Temple area a scant two months before (28:1), Hananiah's death must have caused a sensation (the narrator is careful to note the month). If, by law, a false prophet is to die (Deut. 18:20), and if there is uncertainty about who was the true prophet and who the false, then Yahweh has spoken!

Jeremiah 20:13

Hananiah's death, I suggest, is the background of 20:13. On first reading, this verse seems strangely out of context. We have seen how desperate is the mood of vv. 7–12, and vv. 14–18 are even more desperate. How could Jeremiah give voice to such words of praise as v. 13? But if the words are in response to Hananiah's death, then it is appropriate to "Sing to the Lord; praise the Lord! For he has delivered the life of the needy from the hand of evildoers." This word of triumph reflects some of the language of 15:21, part of Yahweh's earlier reassurance to him, and it makes sense if it is in response to the death of Hananiah.

This understanding of 20:13 suggests the answer to another puzzle which arose earlier regarding the first set of Jeremiah's "confessions" (chap. VIII): Why or how did these private prayers of Jeremiah's become part of the public record of the prophet at all? Now the answer may be clear: Jeremiah publicizes them in order to make clear to others the content of his prayers to Yahweh, prayers for vindication which Yahweh answers in the death of Hananiah. Now Jeremiah knows himself to be vindicated. Now he knows that others must recognize him as a true prophet.

Jeremiah 20:14–18

But, alas, Jeremiah's torment continues, for there is one more lament to Yahweh, in some ways the most terrible of all—20:14–18. And again some phrases need careful examination.

Verse 14 must be understood not as Jeremiah's leveling of a curse on his birth but rather as his declaration that his birth *is already* cursed:

Cursed is the day on which I was born, the day when my mother bore me—how could it be blessed?

Another problem, in vv. 15–17, is the matter of "the man who brought the news to my father" (v. 15). The identity of this man is a puzzle. It might make sense for Jeremiah to level a brief curse at the man in passing, but he continues for line after line, cursing him like Sodom and Gomorrah of old—"the cities that the Lord overthrew" (v. 16). And a man would never have access to the birthing room anyway (vv. 15, 17).

The solution to the puzzle, I propose, is to make a small change and read the verb in the second line of v. 15 as a passive; then we get,

> Cursed is the man about whom my father was brought news: "A son is born to you," a male who did delight him.

That is, Jeremiah is the man; Jeremiah is declaring himself cursed from birth.

> Why did I come forth from the womb to see toil and sorrow and spend my days in shame? (v. 18)

Why, vindicated by Yahweh through the death of Hananiah, does Jeremiah pour out his soul to Yahweh in this heart-rending way? After all, if he was called to be a prophet before his birth (1:5), then he is declaring his very call by Yahweh to be under a curse. This is not blasphemy, but it is the word of a man who has tried to be faithful and has found that now the whole enterprise of faithfulness to Yahweh has come to nothing. It is a word that will later be extended by the poet of the book of Job.[2]

But again, why, given his vindication by Yahweh in the death of Hananiah, does Jeremiah pour out his heart in this way to Yahweh? I suggest that it is because even if Jeremiah is, at least for the moment, vindicated before the crowd at the temple area in Jerusalem, he is far from vindicated before his family. After all, he is doubtless still abstaining from attending weddings and funerals, still a scandal to his people in Anathoth. The fact of his persecution by his family is stated specifically in 12:6, and Jeremiah's reference to his mother in 15:10 is at least suggestive. Further, the phrases here are heavy with references to his mother and his father. There is no way to be certain, but one can imagine that the word in 15:17, "Under the weight of your hand I sat alone," continues to be a description of Jeremiah's relationship with his family.

Why was I ever born? Jeremiah records no answer from God, and the question has resonated for many since Jeremiah's day. We recall Jesus' cry from the cross, "My God, my God, why hast thou forsaken me?" (Mark 15:34), a cry that is the beginning of Psalm 22, a psalm over which Jeremiah must often have brooded (cf. the discussion on pp. 19–20).

We must continue to be astonished at the way in which the book of Jeremiah leads us on beyond the conventional pieties. But there are further surprises ahead: Jeremiah will suddenly begin to preach hope.

NOTES

1. My suggestion cannot be proved. But one may note that the next time "fill" or "full" occurs in Jeremiah (13:12–13), the word is associated with wine. Further, on another occasion Jeremiah describes himself as being "like a drunken man, like a fellow overcome by wine." Others in the Bible who are overcome by religious emotion were accused of being drunk (Hannah, 1 Sam. 1:12–15; those at Pentecost, Acts 2:13).

2. See Job 3, another point at which the book of Job derives themes from Jeremiah; cf. my comments on 12:1 in chap. VIII.

X | TO BUILD AND TO PLANT

Jeremiah had been preaching inevitable doom for twelve years. Suddenly, in 588 B.C.E. he began offering hope, and it all began, I suggest, with his buying a field at his village, Anathoth, an incident narrated in chapter 32.

Jeremiah Buys a Field: Jeremiah 32

Of course "to build and to plant" had been part of Jeremiah's call (1:10), but after King Jehoiakim burned his scroll in 601 B.C.E., he had understood his task to be to "pluck up and to break down" (see chap. II). So he was hardly able even to ponder how his call could include building and planting.

Then suddenly a cousin asked Jeremiah for financial help in keeping ownership of a field at Anathoth within the family. Unfortunately the narrative of the purchase in chapter 32 is heavily overwritten. Commentators conclude that the chapter was expanded by other writers in the century after Jeremiah's time; hence, it is not always easy to discern the original events.[1]

It appears that Hanamel, a cousin of Jeremiah, came to him to ask for help in retaining the ownership of a family field. The law in Lev. 25:25 states that in the event property was in danger of being sold, it was the duty of a near relative to prevent the sale; property should stay in the family.

The time is now six years after the events described here in chapter IX. It is 588 B.C.E. (32:1), and the Babylonian army is besieging Jerusalem for a second time. We shall explore the circumstances in more detail in chapter XI, but it is clear that as the Babylonians renew their attack on the city, Jerusalem's fate will not be pleasant, and Jeremiah continues his preaching of the bad news ahead. Certainly Jeremiah's words could only lower the morale of the troops who were mounting the defense of the city (vv. 2–3). Accordingly King Zedekiah confines him in a "court of the guard." There was no regular prison system in those days, but there was always a way to keep troublemakers in "protective custody."

Jeremiah may have gotten word that his cousin Hanamel was coming on his errand. The narrative as we have it states that word comes to him by divine revelation, and indeed, as it turned out, Jeremiah's purchase of the field is perceived to be at Yahweh's initiative (vv. 6–7).

There is no way to know why Hanamel needed help in retaining the field in the family: he might have gone into debt, or perhaps he decided to sell his holdings in order to migrate to Egypt, out of the way of the disaster that lay ahead. In any event, Hanamel comes to Jeremiah in the court of the guard, and Jeremiah takes on his family obligation, agreeing to buy the field. A natural question is, If Jeremiah has continued to be isolated from his family because of its opposition to his prophesying (see chap. IX), then does he perceive Hanamel's request as an opportunity to be reconciled with his family?

We are given the homely details of the purchase. The price is seventeen shekels of silver (v. 9). Minted coins would not be seen in Palestine until the Persian period, fifty years later; accordingly Jeremiah had to weigh out the pieces of silver for the purchase (v. 10): seventeen shekels is something less than two hundred grams, about six and a half ounces. Conceivably the amount of "seventeen shekels" communicated something specific to people at the time, but whether Jeremiah got a bargain or was being overly generous in the purchase we cannot know. We know neither the purchasing power of silver nor the size of the field.

During this time, Jeremiah's scribe Baruch was either with him or at least within call (v. 12). Was Baruch also being held in the court of the guard with Jeremiah? Baruch must have drawn up the deed at Jeremiah's dictation. There were two copies, the "sealed deed" and the "open copy" (v. 11); these were not two separate pieces of papyrus but a single sheet. The procedure was that the terms of the deed were written out on the top half of the sheet, and then that top half was rolled up, tied, and sealed. Then the terms were written a second time on the bottom half, and the bottom half, or "open copy," was there for all to read. The sealed half at the top was a guarantee that the terms of the bottom half would not be tampered with: if the wording was ever challenged, the top half could be opened for verification.

Jeremiah sees his gesture of buying his cousin's field as a token of personal hope for the future, even though the hope must be deferred; Baruch must, in fact, store the double document in a storage jar for "a long time" (v. 14). Then Jeremiah recognizes clearly that his purchase of the field is not simply an act of family solidarity but a symbolic act done at Yahweh's behest: "Fields shall again be bought in this land" (v. 15).

But this leaves him baffled, and he prays to Yahweh (vv. 16–25). He addresses Yahweh as creator (he is evidently thinking of Yahweh's giving the whole world to Nebuchadrezzar, 27:5; see chap. IX), affirming that "nothing is too hard for you" (v. 17). He recalls that Yahweh rescued Israel from Egypt and brought the people into the land of Canaan (vv. 21–22); Israel disobeyed God and thus brought "all this evil" upon themselves (v. 23). Indeed, Jeremiah goes on, the siege-mounds are now up against the city. The city, faced as it is with sword and famine, is destined to be captured by the Babylonians. Jeremiah's train of thought is: O Lord, you have given me the bad news to preach, and you have brought it to pass, step by step. "What you spoke has happened, as you yourself can see" (v. 24, my trans.). "Yet you, O Lord God, have said to me, 'Buy the field for money and get witnesses'—though the city has been given into the hands of the Chaldeans" (v. 25, NRSV). In other words, Jeremiah says, Lord, finish the job! Why shift your plan right at this point?

Yahweh's answer ironically picks up Jeremiah's word to him in v. 17: "Is anything too hard for me?" (v. 27). Of course there will be punishment (v. 36), but I will gather them from all the lands to which I drove them and bring them back and settle them safely (v. 37). So, yes, the field shall be bought (v. 43, "field" in the Hebrew text is singular) as a sign that fields (plural) will be bought (v. 44).

Here, then, Jeremiah perceives another major shift in Yahweh's will for the people. Until the king burned the prophet's scroll in 601 B.C.E., Yahweh had hoped for repentance from the people. Jeremiah was bidden thereafter to preach bad news. But now, in 588 B.C.E., when the city is under siege and the food supply is dwindling (cf. 37:21), Jeremiah is suddenly bidden by Yahweh to start preaching good news! Yahweh can suddenly change his mind, as we recall from the narrative of Jeremiah's visit to the potter's workshop (see pp. 54–55).

The Scroll of Hope:
Jeremiah 30—31

Where is Jeremiah to begin? When Yahweh's word shifted from the call to repentance to one of irrevocable punishment, Jeremiah could overlay some of the scenarios of possible destruction with firm predictions of that destruction (chap. VII). But there is no way now that Jeremiah can overlay still another layer of material to transform the bad news into good news.

Accordingly, Jeremiah responds to the call from Yahweh in 30:1–3 to write a fresh document that records words of good news:

> For the days are coming when I will restore the fortunes of my people Israel and Judah. (30:3)

So, Jeremiah writes a fresh scroll, which originally contained a good deal of what we now have in chapters 30 and 31.

As a matter of fact, Jeremiah had available to him some oracles of hope from years before. In chapter II, I briefly mentioned traces of early material that the boy Jeremiah directed to the north in the period before 609 B.C.E. (e.g., 3:12–14; 31:4–6); now we must take up the problem again. As we read through chapters 30 and 31, we find evidence of a layer of early poems that Jeremiah had addressed to the now long-dead northern kingdom of Israel. Notice, for example, in 31:5, the reference to "Samaria," the capital of the northern kingdom, and the repeated reference to "Ephraim," one of the chief northern tribes, in 31:6, 9, 18, 20. At the time the poems were first delivered, King Josiah hoped to bring about a reunion with the people in the northern territory upon whom the Assyrian grip was loosening. Jeremiah proclaimed words that both appealed for repentance and promised return from exile (cf. 3:12–14).

Now Jeremiah sees that the old words addressed to the north have a new relevance: the people of Judah must submit to Nebuchadrezzar, but someday they, too, can be called upon to "return" and come back to their land. So Jeremiah takes the old words directed to the north and interweaves them with fresh words to give them relevance to the south. This explains what we have before us in chapters 30 and 31.

According to my understanding, seven passages formed an original cycle of words to the north: (1) 30:5–7; (2) 30:12–15; (3) 30:18–21 and 31:1; (4) 31:2–6 and 9b; (5) 30:15–17; (6) 31:18–20; (7) 31:21–22. The first two of these passages are not, in their original form, words of reassurance at all but words of judgment.

Jeremiah 30:5–7, 10–11

In the first passage, 30:5–7, the people hear shouts of "Terror!" and "No peace!" (v. 5). Yahweh mocks the situation, asking if a male can give birth (v. 6). We must understand that when Yahweh declares holy war, the enemy is demoralized (cf. 6:24). We must also understand that one of the curses leveled against the enemy was, May your warriors turn to women! (Notice the same curse is leveled against Babylon in 50:37 and 51:30.) Here, however, Yahweh is not waging holy war on behalf of Israel against a common enemy. Instead, Yahweh has declared holy war against Yahweh's own people, a cruel irony indeed.

Verse 7 emphasizes the terror of the day when Yahweh's holy war is visited upon the people. The last line of v. 7, as all the translations have it, is a word of hope: "Yet he shall be saved out of it." I suggest, however, that the line was originally heard not as assuring at all but as part of, and in the same mood as, the lines that have preceded it, thus as an ironic question—"And out of it he shall be *saved?*"

But when Jeremiah retrieved this early word to the north and reused it for the south, he added vv. 10–11, words that make the last line of v. 7 a real affirmation of hope. "Yes, he shall be saved out of it: lo, I will save you from afar!" (v. 10). (The prose of vv. 8–9 is a later editorial insertion that breaks up the sequence of poetry.)

Jeremiah 30:12–17

The same process is at work with 30:12–15, an early poem to the north that again offers nothing but judgment. Verses 12–13 use

medical imagery: your hurt is incurable. Verse 14 speaks of guilt
and sins; Yahweh has treated the people as the enemy because of
their guilt. Verse 15 then summarizes the situation, referring both
to "hurt" and "pain" and to "guilt" and "sins," thus rounding off
the poem. But vv. 16–17, Jeremiah's later extension for the south,
speak of a great reversal:

> All who devour you shall be devoured. (v. 16)

and

> I will restore health to you. (v. 17)

Jeremiah 30:18–21; 31:1

By contrast, vv. 18–21 offer a word about restoration. When
v. 18 was directed to the north, it must have led to thoughts of
rebuilding shattered cities there. In its new context it is a wonderful
word for the restoration of Jerusalem. The first part of v. 19 may
refer to songs of joy in the Temple area; the last part affirms that
Yahweh will expand the population once more. Yahweh will punish the oppressor, whether it be Assyria over the north long ago
or Babylon over the south at the moment. In v. 21, "Their prince
shall be one of themselves" would have been heard by the north
as a reference to Josiah (instead of to the Assyrian king). Now, to
the south, it suggests a time when kingship will be reestablished
in Jerusalem.

It appears that vv. 22 and 23–24 are not original here at all: v. 22
is missing in the Septuagint, and vv. 23–24 duplicate 23:19–20,
which is where they really belong. The passage seems to be
rounded off by 31:1, an affirmation that Yahweh will reestablish
covenant with the people once more.

Jeremiah 31:2–9

Both 30:18–21 and 31:2–6 stress rebuilding, but while 30:18–21
deals with "their prince" who "shall be one of themselves" (v. 21),
31:2–6 deals with the unity of worship between north and south:
people in Ephraim (a northern tribe) shall go up to Zion, the hill
of Jerusalem on which the Temple stood (v. 6). This notion of cultic
reunion was part of Josiah's dream. I suggest that 31:2–6 was

originally closed by the last two lines of v. 9, "For I am a father to Israel, and Ephraim is my first-born," an expression parallel to 31:1, which closes 30:18–21.

The phraseology of 31:2–6 plus the last part of v. 9 is thus heavy with references to the north. But when Jeremiah expanded it for the south, he inserted vv. 7–8 and the first part of v. 9: "the land of the north" (v. 8) is Babylon, from which the exiles will come home. In this way the words of v. 6, "Arise, and let us go up to Zion, to the Lord our God," are made relevant to the southerners who return from exile in Babylon.

What Jeremiah has done in v. 8 is fascinating. He has taken words of judgment that are found in 6:21–22 and has turned them backward and inside out. In 6:21 we have "fathers and sons together, neighbor and friend shall perish," while in 31:8 we have "the blind and the lame, the woman with child [i.e., the pregnant woman] and the one in labor, together," images of the handicapped and of women to replace masculine images. In 6:22 we have a description of the Babylonians:

> See, a people is coming from the land of the north,
> a great nation is stirring from the farthest parts of the earth,

while in 31:8 is a description of the exiles coming back from Babylon:

> See, I am going to bring them from the land of the north,
> and gather them from the farthest parts of the earth.

(Verses 10–14 make up a beautiful passage. However, so far as I can see, it is not in Jeremiah's style but is rather a short poem from a century or so later.)

Jeremiah 31:15–17

Verses 15–17 comprise a poignant passage dealing with Rachel and her children. Rachel was the mother of Joseph and therefore the grandmother of Ephraim and Manasseh (Gen. 30:23–24; 41:51–52). Given Jeremiah's preoccupation with "Ephraim" as a symbol for the north, the mention of Rachel here becomes natural. I would reconstruct the last two lines of v. 15 to read,

> She refuses to be consoled: "My babes! My children! Is there none left?"

This verse is well known to Christians through Matthew's use of it in Matt. 2:18 concerning Herod's killing the baby boys in Bethlehem. Here in Jeremiah, however, Rachel's sobbing is relieved by Yahweh's word of restoration in vv. 16–17: her children will come back from the land of the enemy to their own country once more.

Jeremiah 31:18–20

Verses 18–20 are Yahweh's meditation on Ephraim's repentance; the phrases are a wonderful depiction of Yahweh's affection for Ephraim. Some of the wording is difficult. I would translate the verses as follows:

(18) A sound I have heard,
    Ephraim rocking with grief:
"You punished me, and I took the punishment,
    like a calf untrained.
Bring me back, and let me come back,
    for you are Yahweh my God.
(19) For after my captivity I was sorry once more,
    and after I was brought to know, I slapped my thigh.
I was ashamed, even humiliated,
    for I bore the disgrace of my youth."
(20) Is Ephraim a dear son to me,
    a darling child?
For every time I speak of him,
    in fact remember him again,
that is when my very heart trembles for him,
    when in fact I show compassion on him.

We were surprised by expressions in Jeremiah 2 and 3 that implied Yahweh's affection for Israel, and we are surprised again here by these expressions of the depth of Yahweh's love for Ephraim. Yahweh has heard Ephraim sobbing, rocking with grief, penitent, admitting his guilt, accepting his punishment, begging for reconciliation with Yahweh. Yahweh for his part cannot get Ephraim out of his mind and is determined to show compassion to him.

Remember that "Ephraim," that is, the northern kingdom, had disappeared more than a century before this time, and the warm words of Yahweh for this "lost cause" are a reminder to us that

Jeremiah's faith in Yahweh moves far beyond the ordinary predict-abilities of history. As we see him reappropriating the old words now to refer to Judah, we may be reminded that in the context of 588 B.C.E. Babylon would consider Judah too to be a lost cause.

Jeremiah 31:21–22

Verses 21–22 are equally surprising. The address is to the nation personified as female ("O virgin Israel," "O faithless daughter"), but the surprise of the passage in Hebrew is not so apparent in English. Verbs in Hebrew have a distinctive form for the feminine singular, so the commands in v. 21 would be startling: a command to a woman to "set up road markers for yourself," generally piles of stones, and then a command to her to "inspect the highway." All this is ordinarily men's work, and such unexpected commands hint of God's transforming power. This is the reversal of the curse leveled in 30:5–7—that the warriors have become women. If the nation has become feminine, let her take on responsibility for herself; let her note her path to exile so she can retrace her steps.

Then come the final two lines of v. 22: Yahweh has created a "new thing on the earth"—a female encompassing a man. This statement proved so mysterious to St. Jerome in the fourth century that he could understand it only as the Virgin Mary encompassing the Christ child. But no; the statement appears to echo 30:6, "Can a male bear a child?" In that verse we find the word "male," in this verse, the word "female." The nation may have become feminine, but that identity does not have to imply "dilly-dallying" (the meaning of "how long will you waver" at the beginning of 31:22). The nation is in terrible shape, in collapse, but Yahweh in his grace can reshape creation (the verb "created" here is the verb used in Genesis 1) so that the female takes the initiative with the male. Again, as with vv. 18–21, these verses, originally meant for northern Israel, take on a new meaning when the end threatens the city of Jerusalem.

Verses 23–26 of chapter 31 were added much later and are bits and pieces from later writers.

Verses 27–28, I suggest, are the original closing of Jeremiah's scroll of hope, corresponding to the opening in 30:1–3. As for the next two verses (vv. 29–30), though many scholars are convinced that they are original to Jeremiah, my own conclusion is that they are a summary of Ezekiel 18, added by someone a century later.[2] Then the "new covenant" passage, vv. 31–34, is original to Jeremiah. Finally, vv. 35–37 and 38–40 are two passages from a later period that make up an appendix to the new covenant passage.

Verses 31–34, the new covenant passage, attract our particular attention; it is crucial to a study of the book of Jeremiah and is particularly crucial for Christians. The passage, I shall propose, was uttered by Jeremiah after Jerusalem fell to the Babylonians.

The Coming Fall of Babylon: Jeremiah 50—51

Before we take it up, however, it is appropriate to understand how Jeremiah dealt with a question that was urgent when Jerusalem fell: Will Babylon ever fall, and if so, when and how? Jeremiah's poems on this question make up an extended sequence, chapters 50–51. Some of these verses offer a description of the humiliation and fall of Babylon, for example, 50:2, in which the gods of Babylon, Bel and Merodach (Marduk), are put to shame. Other verses are appeals to the Babylonians to flee their city (51:6). But in these verses one hears other messages too—that, for instance, as Babylon falls, Israel will go home (50:4–5, 17a, 19).

The fall of Babylon, according to 50:3 and 9, will occur through a nation out of the north. I have concluded that the original reading of the beginning of v. 9 is "For behold, I am stirring up against Babylon a great company" (by this understanding the words "and bring" and "nations" were expansions by later copyists).[3] Who, in Jeremiah's mind, is this nation from the north?

The key, I suggest, is the repetitive poem in 51:20–23. Most scholars assume that it is Babylon itself that is being addressed here. But there are two problems with this view. First, the beginning of v. 24, "I will repay Babylon and all the inhabitants of Chaldea," parallels closely the phrasing of vv. 20–23. Second, it is certainly not news that by means of Babylon "I [Yahweh] smash nations" (v. 20); Jeremiah had been saying that for years. And there is no other passage in chapters 50–51 in which Yahweh proclaims that Babylon is the instrument of destruction.

The best solution is that Israel itself is Yahweh's "war club and weapon of battle" (51:20) through which Yahweh smashes nations.

Now Jeremiah's conception becomes clear: if Israel is Yahweh's war club and weapon of battle, then Israel is the "nation out of the north" that will come up against Babylon (50:3). Israel is the "great company" whom Yahweh will stir up from the land of the north (50:9). It is no wonder, then, that the announcement that Israel, from the north, will come up against Babylon and make the land a desolation (50:3) is followed by the declaration of the return of the people of Israel and the people of Judah to Zion (50:4–5). What an astonishing reversal that is! Babylon had come upon Israel from the north (4:6; 6:22). Now Israel, having been brought from the north as exiles by Babylon, will be Yahweh's war club against Babylon. The details are spelled out in the reversal mentioned in 30:16:

> All who devour you shall be devoured, and all your foes, every one of them, shall go into captivity; those who plunder you shall be plundered, and all who prey on you I will make a prey.

That image of devouring is extended in the picturesque language of 51:34 and 44.

Years later Babylon finally did fall, but not of course in the way Jeremiah had imagined. It was Cyrus, king of Persia, who came down from the northeast in 538 B.C.E., fifty years later, captured Babylon, and allowed the subject peoples, including Jewish exiles, to return to their homelands. Nevertheless, Jeremiah's visions must have helped sustain the hope of the exiles through their decades of waiting.

The New Covenant:
Jeremiah 31:31–34

Now the New Covenant. If 31:27–28 concluded the original scroll of hope, as I suggested above, then 31:31–34 is an appendix to the scroll. This passage carries great importance for Christians. It is cited in the Epistle to the Hebrews twice, in its entirety in 8:8–12 and in part in 10:16–17, and is thus worth examining in some detail.

We have assumed here the year 588 B.C.E. was when Jeremiah began proclaiming hope to his people. The Babylonian siege of Jerusalem continued into the following year. The city fell to the besiegers in July of 587 B.C.E. (39:2 = 2 Kings 25:3), and in August of that year the Babylonian army commander burned the Temple, the palace, and the main houses, and destroyed the defense wall of the city (2 Kings 25:8–10; for more detail, see chap. IX). Then, the end of September or beginning of October of 587 B.C.E. was the occasion once more for reading aloud the law of Deuteronomy (cf. the mention in chap. IX of the occasion seven years before, in 594 B.C.E.). It is hard to imagine that the priests would still follow the custom since the Temple was now destroyed, but they may have felt all the more impelled to do so as a gesture of continuity with the past. I propose that reading of Deuteronomy as the setting for 31:31–34, Jeremiah's proclamation of the new covenant.

Jeremiah had already proposed one "new thing" that God would do (31:22); here is another even more surprising new thing. On first reading the passage seems easy to understand. The time is coming when God will make a new covenant with Israel and Judah, one that resembles the old one in some respects but contrasts with it in other crucial respects. The difference between the two covenants is that next time God will put the law within the people, so that overt instruction will no longer be necessary.

In both the RSV and NRSV, the passage is printed as prose in Jeremiah but, paradoxically, as poetry in its citation in Heb. 8:8–12. I understand the passage in Jeremiah to fall into two halves, the first of which (ending in v. 33 with "after those days, says the Lord") is in prose, the second in poetry. The prose section describes, in the style of Deuteronomy, the old black-and-white days of the old covenant; the poetic section describes the new technicolor days of the new covenant.

The first section, though in prose, has a careful structure, beginning and ending with the word "days" (in vv. 31, 33), continuing inward with "I will make a new covenant with the house of Israel" (v. 31) and "this is the covenant I will make with the house of Israel" (v. 33), and continuing further inward with two references to the old covenant, "the covenant I made with their ancestors" and "my covenant that they broke" (v. 32). This leads to the center—the mention of God's act of saving the people from Egypt: "when I took them by the hand to bring them out of the land of Egypt" (v. 32). (See Figure 2.) (Jeremiah slips in a

A   (31) The *days* are surely coming, says the Lord,

  B   when *I will make* a new *covenant with the house of Israel* and the house of Judah.

    C   (32) It will not be like the *covenant that I made with their ancestors*

      D   when I took them by the hand *to bring them out of the land of Egypt—*

    C   *a covenant that they broke,* though I was their husband, says the Lord.

  B   (33) But this is the *covenant that I will make with the house of Israel*

A   after those *days,* says the Lord.

Figure 2

surprise here, though, adding, "though I was their husband," using the same verb derived from "baal" that he used in 3:14; see chap. IV.)

The poetic section (vv. 33b–34) is shaped with equal care, beginning with two first-person singular verbs, "I will put my law within them, and I will write it on their hearts" (v. 33), and closing likewise with two first-person singular verbs, "I will forgive their iniquity, and remember their sin no more" (v. 34). This encloses the covenantal formula "I will be their God, and they shall be my people" and the lines about the lack of necessity for overt teaching (v. 34).

The implication here is that the old covenant is dead because it has been thoroughly violated by the people, and therefore that the exercise of rereading Deuteronomy—if that is actually the context for this passage—is futile indeed. But if the old covenant is dead, God can draw up a new covenant without the loopholes of the old one—as if God had learned a thing or two from the experience of the first, failed version. The old covenant was written on tablets of stone—the Ten Commandments. The new covenant, by contrast, will be written inside people, on the "heart." The word "heart" is singular in Hebrew and refers, we recall, to the character, the seat of decision making. Next time around, the people will obey God not because they are supposed to but because they want to;

awareness of God will not be something externally taught but internally natural.

Jeremiah had once, at the time of his call, thought himself to be the prophet like Moses (see chap. II). Then, when he was forbidden to intercede for his people, he became an anti-Moses figure (see chap. VII). Now once more he becomes the prophet like Moses, the announcer (if not the mediator) of a fresh covenant between God and the people.

This astonishing vision, as we have noted, became an appendix to the scroll of hope. It is striking, though, that it is never referred to again in the Old Testament. Indeed, the prophet fifty years later who wrote, "The word of our God stands for ever" (Isa. 40:8) seems in his way to be contradicting it.

The passage was reappropriated only centuries later by two groups of people. The first group was the Dead Sea Scroll community, who understood *themselves* to be the people of the new covenant; the phrase appears several times in their scrolls. The second group was the followers of Jesus of Nazareth, who remembered his having said, at the time of his last supper with his disciples, "This cup is the new covenant in my blood" (Luke 22:20). For Christians, then, the passage became the basis for Christian self-understanding, as we have already seen in the quotation of the passage in the letter to the Hebrews.

And indeed there is that wonderful sense of divine breakthrough in the pages of the book of Acts, that conviction that God has taken the initiative in Jesus to free men and women from all that hinders them in responding to God. St. Augustine, in the fourth century, caught the spirit when he wrote, "Love God, and do what you like," meaning not that Christians are free to do absolutely anything at all, but simply that if Christians really love God, then to "do what you like" is to do what God wills. Christians look to the prayer of Jesus in the Garden of Gethsemane, "Father, if thou art willing, remove this cup from me; nevertheless not my will, but thine, be done" (Luke 22:42), as a point where God's law was put within the human heart, and Christians cling to that possibility for themselves.

One might object, of course, that Jeremiah's vision has not quite been achieved (cf. 31:34), inasmuch as the process of religious instruction is still very much with us. But such an objection only dramatizes the innovation of Jeremiah's vision of hope. Here, as in so much else, he was the most unconventional of prophets.

NOTES

1. For commentaries in English, see conveniently J. Philip Hyatt, "Exegesis of Jeremiah," *The Interpreter's Bible* (New York and Nashville: Abingdon Press, 1956), 5:1042–43; and John Bright, *Jeremiah*, Anchor Bible (Garden City, N.Y.: Doubleday & Co., 1965), 298.

2. The style of the verses is not that of Jeremiah: the phrase "die for one's own sin" is not appropriate to Jeremiah but is common in Ezekiel (see Ezek. 3:18, 19). Furthermore, other passages in Jeremiah that speak of a change of speech-pattern (3:16; 23:7–8) betray a late date.

3. The history of the text is complicated. See my *Jeremiah 2*, Hermeneia (Minneapolis: Augsburg Fortress, 1989), 392, 416.

THE FALL OF JERUSALEM, AND THE PASSION OF JEREMIAH

For most of Jeremiah's career we have had to be content with bits and pieces—the scene of Jeremiah's trial after the Temple Sermon (chap. III), the scene of Jeremiah's dictating a scroll to Baruch (chap. V), King Jehoiakim burning the scroll (chap. VII), Jeremiah's confrontation with Hananiah (chap. VIII), and the like, and we have had to surmise the developments between these scenes. However, for the period from roughly the spring of 588 B.C.E. to the fall of 587 B.C.E. we have a more continuous narrative of what happened to the prophet, a narrative given to us in chapters 37–44. This narrative is so complete because the narrator, evidently Jeremiah's scribe Baruch, wished particularly to record what happened to Jeremiah before and after the fall of Jerusalem.

The eight chapters appear to fall into two unequal sections. The first and longer section, 37:1—43:3, takes the story of Jeremiah from the first time King Zedekiah consulted him and asked him to pray for the people (37:3) to the time after the fall of Jerusalem when a little military group that stopped at Bethlehem asked Jeremiah to pray for them (42:2). The second, shorter, section is a kind of appendix and takes the story of Jeremiah from Bethlehem to Egypt (43:4—44:30).

Jeremiah in the Collapse of Jerusalem: Jeremiah 37:1—43:3

The first section offers an opening scene, in which there is a request to "pray for us" (37:3–10), and a closing scene offering a request to "pray for us" (42:1—43:3). Between these two scenes are six other scenes, each of which is closed by the statement "and

Jeremiah stayed" at a given place (37:16, 21; 38:13, 28; 39:14; 40:6). The same Hebrew verb *yāshab* is translated either "remained" or "stayed" in these verses.

Jeremiah 37:3–10

In the first scene King Zedekiah sends a delegation to ask for Jeremiah's intercession for the people. The situation at that time was already grim: in January 588 B.C.E. the Babylonians began the second siege of Jerusalem (see 2 Kings 25:1). Jeremiah may already have been confined in the court of the guard, during which time he arranged for the purchase of the field at Anathoth. In 37:5 we learn almost in passing that the Egyptians sent an army to drive the Babylonians away, a project that succeeded for the moment; this must have been in the spring or early summer of 588 B.C.E.

Six years before, remember, Jeremiah had interrupted King Zedekiah's summit conference with his own dark word, an interruption that cannot have endeared him to the king (chap. IX). Why at this point, then, would the king send a delegation to Jeremiah to ask for help? There is no way to know. In these chapters, the king is not depicted as strong, and it is altogether likely that he has been consulting an array of prophets, trying to piece together as much information as he can. Perhaps word has come to him that Jeremiah has begun to preach good news. In any event, the king does consult him, and the answer he gets is the same old answer: Egypt will retreat, and Babylon will renew the siege and take the city.

Jeremiah 37:11–16

In the second scene Jeremiah tries, during this break in the siege of the city, to go north, in all likelihood to claim ownership of the field he had bought from his cousin. But as he goes out of one of the city gates, he is arrested by the officer in charge and accused of desertion to the Babylonians: Jeremiah's conviction that the fall of the city of Babylon is inevitable must have been well known in the city. Though Jeremiah denies the charge, the officials become enraged at him and shut him up in the house of a scribe named Jonathan, which had been made into a prison (37:13–15). Jeremiah remains there for a long time (the implication of "many days" in v. 16).

Jeremiah 37:17–21

In the third scene King Zedekiah sends for Jeremiah, who is brought from prison to the palace. It is likely by this time that the Egyptians have withdrawn and the Babylonians have renewed their hold around the city. This time the king speaks to Jeremiah personally, though secretly. The meeting certainly suggests that the king is specifically concerned about what Jeremiah can tell him; he is not simply interested in canvassing prophetic opinion. He asks if there is any word from Yahweh. There is, of course, but it is the same old word—the king will be delivered into the hand of the king of Babylon.

And then come three verses, 37:18–20, in which we suddenly hear Jeremiah in a new role, not an awesome prophet for Yahweh nor a prophet seemingly abandoned by Yahweh, but simply a vulnerable human being, addressing the king about his mistreatment. "What have I done wrong, to you or anyone else, that I should be put into prison? And where are your good-news prophets who told you Nebuchadrezzar would not come back?"—for there must have been many others who shared Hananiah's outlook (see chap. IX). "Let me humbly ask not to be sent back to the house of Jonathan to die there." Accordingly, King Zedekiah, who is clearly working at cross-purposes with his officials, has Jeremiah committed to the court of the guard and makes sure that Jeremiah receives a daily ration of bread so long as the bread supply holds out. But it is a slim ration; the "loaf" of bread is literally a "disk" of bread, one piece of something like modern pita bread.

Jeremiah 38:1–13

In the fourth scene, 38:1–13, the officials once more take the initiative with Jeremiah, who is evidently able to get word to the people that whoever surrenders will survive but the city will inevitably fall to the Babylonians. The officials want to execute Jeremiah, and the king gives in to them and says, "Here he is, he is in your hands" (v. 5). They drop Jeremiah into a cistern, the bottom of which is muddy (v. 6). The cisterns of the time were typically shaped like a huge bottle, with a large diameter but only a small opening at the top, which was often covered with a stone. There would be no way, therefore, for Jeremiah to climb out, and the mud at the bottom would allow him no secure footing, so that he would not be able to survive too long.

At this point an Ethiopian servant of the king intervenes. The servant's name is given as "Ebed-melech," which in Hebrew means simply "king's servant": the kind of name people would give a foreigner whose real name they could not pronounce. This foreigner, astonishingly, confronts the king with boldness when none of Jeremiah's fellow citizens do. When Ebed-melech hears that Jeremiah has been dropped into the muddy cistern, he goes down from the palace to the gate on the north side of the city where the king is sitting and confronts him. The Septuagint reading of v. 9 is probably correct: "You have done wrong in what you did, to try to kill this man." And as astonishing as the servant's boldness is the king's lack of anger, indeed, his positive response. Out of earshot of his officials, the king can countermand their act; he tells Ebed-melech to get three men and rescue Jeremiah. Accordingly, the servant goes to a storeroom in the palace and gets some clothing scraps so that when ropes are lowered to Jeremiah, the prophet can protect his arms as he is pulled up. Imagine the turmoil of Jeremiah's thoughts as he is pulled from the cistern and what would have surely been a grotesque death. And then he is sent back to the court of the guard!

Jeremiah 38:14–27; 39:15–18; 38:28

The fifth scene comprises the rest of chapter 38. I propose, however, that the last four verses of chapter 39 are misplaced and that they originally came between 38:27 and 28. I include them in this scene, whose order therefore is 38:14–27 + 39:15–18 + 38:28.

In this episode King Zedekiah makes yet a third inquiry of Jeremiah. The relationship between the two is strange: the king, who presumably has all the power and whom Jeremiah has treated respectfully (37:20) but who cannot face down his own officials in their opposition to Jeremiah (38:5), on the one hand, and Jeremiah, upon whom the king seems dependent for advice but who is being variously restricted, on the other. The king's conversation with

Ebed-melech had certainly been public (38:7–10), but this conversation is private (38:27). The "third entrance to the temple," where they meet, may have been a private entrance for the king.

In any event, in response to the king's question Jeremiah reiterates the old word from God. The king then most surprisingly opens his heart to Jeremiah, leading Jeremiah in turn to move from his former courtesy to greater frankness. The king begins, "I have something to ask you; do not hide anything from me" (38:14). Jeremiah's reply is, "If I tell you, you will put me to death, will you not? and if I give you advice, you will not listen to me" (38:15, NRSV). The king then swears to him, "As the Lord lives, who gave us our lives, I will not put you to death or hand you over to these men who seek your life" (38:16, NRSV). Jeremiah then explains as before, If you surrender to Babylon, you will save your life, and the city will be spared; but if you do not surrender, the city will be burned, and you will not escape (38:17–18).

Then the king unburdens himself, confessing his fear of those in the city who have already deserted to the Babylonians, his fear that he might fall into their hands and be mistreated (38:19). The king has status now, but if he surrenders, he will be just one more refugee, stripped of his privileges and open to the taunts of earlier deserters, who might well be opportunists, who are now pro-Babylonian and could view the king as an enemy prisoner of war, and who might very well resent the king's holding out as long as he does.

Jeremiah reassures the king that his fear is an empty one, but he goes on to share with him a vision he has had of the women of the palace taunting their king as they are led out to captivity: "They've led you off and overcome you, your fine friends; they got your foot stuck in the mud and then drew back" (38:22, my trans.). Here is a potential source of taunting for the king that is closer at hand! We are not told how the king reacts to this bit of news, but he does arrange for a cover story in case Jeremiah is subsequently questioned by the officials (38:24–26), a cover story Jeremiah later needs to use and uses successfully (38:27).

Then we are told that Jeremiah hears from Yahweh a word of reassurance to Ebed-melech, the servant who has pulled him out of the muddy cistern: in all the terrible events ahead Ebed-melech will escape at least with his life (39:15–18). But Jeremiah himself remained in the court of the guard until Jerusalem fell (38:28).

Jeremiah 39:1–3; 39:11–14

The sixth scene narrates the fall of Jerusalem (39:1–3) and Nebuchadrezzar's command to his senior officer to protect Jeremiah (39:11–14). Jeremiah 39:4–10 has been inserted into this sequence. These verses are a summary of 52:7–16; they are not in the Septuagint and do not deal with Jeremiah but are concerned with the fate of King Zedekiah.

The food supply ran out (52:6), and the city fell in July 587 B.C.E., as we noted in chapter X. The king and his immediate family and retainers attempted to escape the city, perhaps hoping to take refuge with the Ammonite king (cf. 40:14), but Babylonian forces captured them near Jericho and took them north to Nebuchadrezzar's field headquarters in Syria. There Nebuchadrezzar imposed brutal sentences on them. He executed the king's sons and nobility and blinded the king and took him in chains to Babylon (39:4–7; 52:7–11). The Septuagint text of 52:11 specifies that he was put in the "house of milling" till the day of his death, that is, he did women's work, which calls to mind Samson's fate in Judg. 16:21.

The next month the senior Babylonian officer, named Nebuzaradan, entered the city and burned the Temple, the palace, and the main houses of the city. He demolished the defense wall of the city and rounded up the chief citizens for deportation to Babylon (39:8–10; 52:12–15).

As we have noted, Jeremiah had remained in the court of the guard (38:28; 39:14). The narrative says that Nebuzaradan had received an order from Nebuchadrezzar to take care of Jeremiah: "Take him and look after him; do not do any harm to him, but whatever he says to you, do with him" (39:12). It is not impossible that Jeremiah really was known in the Babylonian camp and that such orders really had been given; there were, after all, deserters who may have spoken of him (38:19). Accordingly, Nebuzaradan entrusts him to Gedaliah (39:14), a member of the class of officials and the one whom Nebuchadrezzar will soon appoint governor over Judah (40:7). At this point then, Jeremiah is free to come and go as he pleases (39:14). It is worth noting that Gedaliah's father,

Ahikam, had protected Jeremiah twenty-two years before at the time of the prophet's Temple Sermon (26:24).

Jeremiah 40:1–6

The seventh scene covers 40:1–6. Unfortunately the text of vv. 2–3 has become muddled; I propose that the first part of v. 2 ("The captain of the guard took Jeremiah and said to him") belongs after v. 3. In spite of the fact that Nebuzaradan has allowed Jeremiah to go free, the prophet has evidently been caught in a later roundup and put in chains at Ramah, part of a group of people destined for deportation. By my proposal, the words of the quotation in vv. 2–3, beginning, "The Lord your God pronounced evil against this place," are words that Jeremiah addresses to his *fellow prisoners*.[1] The words of the quotation that continues in v. 4 through the middle of v. 5 are obviously spoken by Nebuzaradan to Jeremiah: the officer catches up with the prophet and releases him from his chains, offering him the choice of going to Babylon as a free man or staying in Judah in the care of Gedaliah. Jeremiah chooses the latter.

Jeremiah 40:7—43:3

The eighth and last scene narrates Jeremiah's time with a band of refugees under the command of a Jewish officer named Johanan. The immediate scene is narrated in 42:1—43:3 but has a lengthy introduction that explains the circumstances (40:7—41:18).

The circumstances were these. Though Jerusalem could no longer serve as the capital, there had to be some kind of central seat of authority. Accordingly Nebuchadrezzar appointed Gedaliah to be governor and installed him at Mizpah, a high point just north of Jerusalem (40:7–8), with a garrison of Babylonian soldiers (cf. 41:3). Nebuzaradan had entrusted to Gedaliah's care not only people like Jeremiah but others who were not destined for deportation (40:8), including, curiously, some princesses (cf. 41:10 and 43:6).

When Gedaliah's appointment as governor becomes known, various military officers in the field begin to come to Gedaliah with their men to assess the situation (40:7–8). Gedaliah swears to these officers that he will represent the Jewish population to the Babylonians and that he will guarantee the safety of the military men who come before him. He urges them during the weeks of late summer and early fall to get the crops in so that they and their villages can survive, and that word goes out (40:9–12).

One of the officers, Johanan, becomes their spokesman. He warns Gedaliah that Baalis, the Ammonite king across the Jordan, is sponsoring what we would today call a freedom fighter, a man named Ishmael who is a member of the royal family of Judah (41:1), and that Baalis is sending Ishmael to assassinate Gedaliah as a collaborator. Gedaliah, however, does not believe him (40:13–14). Johanan then speaks to Gedaliah privately, offering to kill Ishmael. But Gedaliah will not hear of it (40:15–16), perhaps out of respect for someone of royal blood.

In late September or early October Ishmael comes to Gedaliah in Mizpah with ten of his men, and Gedaliah receives them for a meal (41:1). Hospitality in the Near East is a matter of honor and Gedaliah is obligated to protect his guests. But Johanan's warning proves right after all: Ishmael and his men betray the hospitality they are enjoying. They assassinate Gedaliah, and his Jewish retainers and the Babylonian guard (41:2–3) as well, so that there are no witnesses to speak of the atrocity. There are, however, still civilians nearby who have been under Gedaliah's care (see 41:10), including Jeremiah (cf. 42:2; 43:6) and Baruch (cf. 43:3).

The situation becomes more complicated the next day when a band of eighty pilgrims comes down the road from Shechem and Samaria in the north, intending to offer sacrifices in Jerusalem. They are in mourning for the destroyed Temple, their beards shaved, their clothes torn, and their bodies gashed (41:4–5). Since it is the month for the festival of booths and the occasion for reciting Deuteronomy, that may be the occasion that brings them south to Jerusalem. Ishmael must have seen from a distance the dust rising from the pilgrim procession, and may have thought that word of the slaughter had gotten out after all and that the pilgrims were a military expedition against him. At any rate, with utter insincerity he goes out to meet them, sharing their weeping and inviting them in on the pretense that they should accept Gedaliah's hospitality (41:6). When the group comes in to Mizpah, Ishmael kills them as well. Ten of the group are able to bribe their way out, but the rest are slaughtered and their bodies thrown into a local cistern (41:7–9). Ishmael and his men then gather up all the civilians who have been under Gedaliah's care, including the princesses and Jeremiah and Baruch, and move off to the north, doubtless intending to return across the Jordan to the protection of the Ammonite king (41:10).

Johanan, who tried to warn Gedaliah of Ishmael's plot, hears of the massacre and attempts to catch up with Ishmael's band. He comes upon them at Gibeon and rescues the civilians, much to their relief, but Ishmael and eight of his men manage to slip away to the Ammonites—he has lost two of his men along the way (41:11–15)!

Johanan and his men take charge of the band of civilians and move south, intending to get to Egypt, where they will be away from the skirmishes between freedom fighters and collaborators. They stop for the moment at a caravan resting place near Bethlehem (41:16–18). It is interesting to speculate. As they passed through Jerusalem, did Jeremiah deliver the words of the "new covenant" passage (31:31–34; see chap. X)? It is certainly possible.

Now Jeremiah emerges in the group. His status and freedom to leave the group are unclear. But what is clear is that for the moment there is anarchy in Judah. Furthermore, Jeremiah is well known and widely thought to have collaborated with the Babylonians (cf. 37:13; 39:11–12; 40:4). Surely he is tired of being under threat of death. In these circumstances he might well prefer having a military protector to being on his own.

In this eighth scene Johanan asks Jeremiah to pray for the little band and to ask Yahweh for guidance (42:1–3). This raises a question: If Johanan has intended to go to Egypt all along (41:17), why does he bother to ask Jeremiah for Yahweh's guidance? Perhaps the group suddenly felt itself vulnerable ("for we are left but a few out of many," 42:2), and some of the civilians may have started murmuring to their officers. The question may have crossed Jeremiah's mind, too, given the way the matter turns out (cf. 43:1–3), but he agrees to pray to Yahweh for guidance for the group (42:4). The group agrees to abide by the word that Jeremiah receives (42:5–6).

It takes a full ten days for Jeremiah to receive an answer (42:7);

the prophet cannot expect to receive an answer from God quickly. Imagine how many times during those ten days Johanan must have asked Jeremiah, "Is there a word from the Lord?" (cf. 37:17). But the answer when it does come is, If you change your mind and decide to stay in this land, then Yahweh will suddenly build and plant, not uproot and tear down, and you need have no fear of Nebuchadrezzar (42:10-12). But if you are determined to go to Egypt, then you will know nothing but sword and famine (42:13-17).

I suggest that 43:1-3 belongs here, directly after 42:17. In 43:1-3 the officers renege on their agreement (see 42:6) and begin to argue with Jeremiah and, amusingly, to blame Baruch for this word, doubting that it has any divine origin at all. Following this, Jeremiah reiterates Yahweh's word: "Yahweh has said to you, do not go to Egypt" (42:19). Jeremiah says that he has done just what they told him to do, namely, consult Yahweh (42:18-22).

Prophetic Words from Egypt

What follows now is the second, shorter section of chapters 37—44, a kind of appendix that narrates Jeremiah's stay in Egypt. The appendix begins with the brief notice in 43:4-7 that the group did go south to Egypt and that the group in particular included Jeremiah and Baruch. They settled for the moment in Tahpanhes, a city in the Nile Delta (see 2:16). At this point we lose track of Johanan and the other officers; we are given three narratives in which Jeremiah offers prophetic words.

Jeremiah 43:8-13

The first of these prophetic words occurs at Tahpanhes (43:8-13), where Jeremiah performs a symbolic action: He buries several large stones in the pavement in front of the government building in Tahpanhes (43:9). As he does so, he offers a divine word: Nebuchadrezzar will come even to Egypt and will set up his throne here on these stones, destroying as he does so, burning the temples of the Egyptian gods (43:10-12). The key verb in the second half of verse 12, 'aṭā, has two meanings, "wrap oneself with" and "delouse," so Nebuchadrezzar will both *wrap himself* with the land of Egypt and *delouse* Egypt, as a shepherd delouses a cloak, and, having done so, he will go away again unscathed. So much for the vaunted pomp and circumstance of Egypt! Nebuchadrezzar actually did lead a successful raid into Egypt some twenty years later.

Jeremiah 44:1–25

The second section of the appendix, 44:1–25, is an interchange between Jeremiah and all the Jews in Egypt, both those in the Nile Delta area (Tahpanhes and Migdol) and those in southern Egypt (Pathros). Jeremiah and Baruch may have moved on from Tahpanhes, but the narrative does not indicate their location. Jeremiah addresses the Jews about their worship of the "queen of heaven" (44:1–14). First the men answer him (44:15–18), and then the women do (44:19). Jeremiah then answers the men (44:20–23) and the women (44:24–25), though the text has been rewritten so it is at some points difficult to distinguish between the sections referring to the men and those referring to the women.

Jeremiah insists that the fall of Jerusalem came about because the inhabitants worshiped other gods (44:2–6), and that a similar disaster will come upon those from Judah who have settled in Egypt (44:7–10): why do you continue to do a great evil?

The men answer Jeremiah (44:15–18), referring to "the queen of heaven," Astarte (see chaps. IV and VII). They know, of course, that their wives have worshiped Astarte (44:15), and the men freely admit that they do too, convinced that when they worshiped Astarte, their fields were fertile and they had plenty to eat, whereas when they stopped worshiping her they starved and were destroyed by the sword (44:17–18). The women then speak up (44:19), reinforcing their husbands' choice: of course they worship Astarte; they have done so with their husbands' approval.

Jeremiah's view of "sacred history" is thus challenged by his audience's contrasting view of "sacred history." Jeremiah's view, in effect, is that when King Josiah reformed the cult in 622 B.C.E. they stood a chance of survival, but after Josiah died in 609 B.C.E. and the reform lapsed, there has been nothing but disaster. But the view held by the Jews in Egypt is, in effect, that when King Josiah got rid of the fertility gods in 622 B.C.E. he set the stage for disaster. He was struck down in the prime of life, killed in battle when he was thirty-eight years old. Whose view of history is right?

Jeremiah has no answer to the men except to reiterate his own understanding of history with even more passion (44:20–23). In 44:21 he really means, Has not the sacrificing which you did in the cities of Judah and in the streets of Jerusalem, you and your fathers, your kings and your officials, and the people of the land, been remembered by Yahweh, and has it not come to Yahweh's mind? Nor has he an answer for the women except to concede to them their choice and to address them sarcastically, saying, in effect, You have spoken with your mouths and have done it with your hands, saying, "We really will perform our vows"; so of course, go ahead and confirm your vows and perform them (44:24–25).

Jeremiah 44:26–30

Jeremiah's final address to the Jews in Egypt is recorded in 44:26–30. In it the central issue is the use in Egypt of God's name "Yahweh." Jeremiah had once thought himself to be the prophet like Moses (see chap. II). Then when he was bidden by God not to pray for the people he became an anti-Moses figure (see chap. VII). Then in announcing the new covenant, he once more became the prophet like Moses (see chap. X). Now, finally, he is the supreme anti-Moses figure: instead of leading the people out of Egypt, he himself has been led by the people back to Egypt. All Jeremiah can do is proclaim that the name "Yahweh," announced to Moses in Egypt (Exod. 3:14), is no longer to be invoked by the Jews in Egypt. It is the end of at least this portion of Yahweh's great experiment.

Conclusion

This is the last glimpse we have of Jeremiah. We have no notice of how his days ended, how he died, or where he was buried. Since Baruch had evidently been recording this account, we can only assume that Baruch died first, leaving Jeremiah without anyone to complete the written story.

It is an astonishing concluding narrative. Jerusalem is under siege and then falls, and what follows is chaos. What befalls Jeremiah in the midst of that chaos is narrated in detail. He is kept moving here and there, caught up in the swirl of events. The palace officials falsely accuse him of desertion and put him in prison, but the king releases him to the court of the guard. Then the officials throw him into a muddy cistern. Then again the king agrees to have him pulled out and reassigned to the court of the guard, where he stays until the city falls. Though specifically singled out for protection by the Babylonian officer in charge, he nevertheless finds himself shackled along with other citizens waiting to be deported. He is suddenly released by the Babylonian officer once more and entrusted to the governor in Mizpah. But when the governor is assassinated, he finds himself along with others taken as a hostage by the assassin Ishmael, who intends to take the group across the Jordan to the Ammonites. But the hostages are suddenly rescued in Gibeon by Johanan, taken back to Mizpah, and then quickly moved on to Bethlehem. Eventually Jeremiah is moved down to Egypt along with the others, and there we finally lose sight of him.

In a way Jeremiah's is a kind of passion narrative analogous to the passion narratives of Jesus in the Gospels, but without the kind of resolution that the narratives of the resurrection afford. There is never any suggestion in the course of the narration that "the hand of Yahweh was with Jeremiah" in any of these events (cf. 36:26), nor is there any happy outcome suggested from Jeremiah's suffering. The narrative does not glorify Jeremiah or his endurance.[2]

On the other hand, through all these changes of fortune, Jeremiah is portrayed as an active mediator for the word of Yahweh. Jeremiah is a prisoner when King Zedekiah seeks him out for the third time, and yet, curiously, Jeremiah seems to be freer than the king. He continues to speak out the word of Yahweh, simply, quietly, firmly, while the king betrays his weakness and his fears.[3]

This word of Yahweh cuts across all the human expectations of those around Jeremiah. "Surrender to Babylon and live!" "Stay in Judah: there is no safety in Egypt!" And in no single instance does Jeremiah have any reassurance that anyone is listening—except Baruch, who writes it all down. That the basket of scrolls will be saved and used after his death, that in Egypt two and a half centuries later his words will be translated into Greek, that his words will be meditated upon by the Dead Sea Scroll community in the wilderness of Judea five centuries later, that his words will become part of the Scripture of the peoples of the covenant and be pondered from one end of the world to the other—all this is completely beyond his ken. Surely "God chose what is foolish in the world to shame the wise, God chose what is weak in the world to shame the strong, God chose what is low and despised in the world, even things that are not, to bring to nothing things that are, so that no human being might boast in the presence of God" (1 Cor. 1:27–29).[4]

NOTES

1. The second-person references in v. 3 are plural in Hebrew.

2. See Gerhard von Rad, *Old Testament Theology* (New York: Harper & Row, 1965), 2:207–8.

3. Cf. Benhard Duhm, *Das Buch Jeremia* (Tübingen: J.C.B. Mohr, 1901), 301.

4. Some of the phrasing of this conclusion has been adapted from my *Jeremiah 2*, Hermeneia (Minneapolis: Augsburg Fortress, 1989), 305–6. Used by permission.

XII | PROPHET OUT OF TIME

Summing up the importance of Jeremiah involves two tasks, one simpler and one more complicated.

Jeremiah within the Tradition of Old Testament Prophets

The first task, the simpler one, is to determine how Jeremiah fits into the whole tradition in which he stands.

Jeremiah stood in the long line of Old Testament prophets. He drew from Hosea in his metaphor of Israel as the bride of Yahweh; and he drew many of his phrases from Amos, Hosea, and Isaiah, from narratives about creation and the patriarchs in Genesis, and from narratives of Moses and Samuel. In this way he sums up richly the tradition of his people up to his time.

At the same time, many later bodies of material drew on the phrases of Jeremiah. Ezekiel's vision of eating a scroll (Ezek. 2:8—3:3), for example, is dependent on Jer. 15:16, "Thy words were found, and I ate them." The prophet who wrote Isaiah 40—55 also drew on Jeremiah; for example, the figure of the suffering servant in Isa. 52:13—53:12 rests partly on Jeremiah's personal experience (cf. Isa. 53:7 with Jer. 11:19). The poet who wrote the poem of Job drew from Jeremiah; Job 3, for example, is evidently an expansion of Jer. 20:14–18; and the metaphor of Job's legal struggle with God, found in Job 9, is dependent on Jer. 12:1–3.

Jesus also drew on Jeremiah. He used the "den of robbers" phrase from Jeremiah's Temple Sermon (7:11) when in his day he turned the money changers out of the Temple (see chap. III). And Jesus' cry of dereliction on the cross, "My God, my God, why have you forsaken me?" echoes Jeremiah's sense of abandonment by God (see chap. IX). Indeed, one could say that Jeremiah was an explorer of the way of the cross, an unwilling explorer, perhaps, but one nonetheless—and even Jesus is recorded as praying in the garden of Gethsemane: "Remove this cup from me" (Mark 14:36). The tradition that Matthew reports—that some thought that Jesus was Jeremiah come to life again (Matt. 16:14)—reflects an acute awareness of the resemblance between the two.

In passing, I may suggest that if we ever have occasion to wonder about the nature of Jesus' own inner life, his own self-understanding, then we might well find indirect but suggestive resources in the story of Jeremiah, who anticipated him in so many ways. Jesus evidently included "prophet" among the categories he applied to himself (see Mark 6:4 and Luke 13:32–35), and the insight that we gain into the inner life of Jeremiah may give resonance to our understanding of Jesus.

Paul likewise reflected more than once on the material of Jeremiah. Think, for example, of the resemblance between Gal. 1:15, "But when he who had set me apart before I was born, and had called me through his grace," and the opening words of Jeremiah's call in Jer. 1:5. The epistle to the Hebrews takes over the whole of the "new covenant" passage and makes Christian testimony out of it (see chap. X). The book of Revelation is crowded with reminiscences of the book of Jeremiah: the "springs of living water" (Rev. 7:17), to cite just one passage, is plainly a reflection of Jer. 2:13.

Thus not only did the book of Jeremiah itself become Scripture for later generations but the words of that book themselves gave rise to many fresh expressions in the words of later generations, words that then in their turn became Scripture. Thus even though during his own lifetime Jeremiah may have thought of himself as socially isolated ("I sat alone," 15:17), in the long run he emerges as part of a consistent company that spans many centuries of the biblical tradition.

A Prophet for Today

The second task in summing up is to ask whether God speaks to us now through Jeremiah, and if so, how. In this volume, I have avoided making statements such as, "God speaks through Jeremiah." Instead, up to this point I have assumed that it is more useful to make such statements as "Jeremiah was convinced that God spoke through him to his people." My steady use of the name "Yahweh" serves the same purpose. All this may seem cumbersome, but there is a reason for it.

Until this point I have looked at Jeremiah as I might look at any other figure whose life and teachings have had an impact on the world—Socrates, or Joan of Arc, or Gandhi. I have tried to acquaint readers with his story so that they become involved in it and can react positively to it. My goals have been to allow for appreciation of a fellow human being, to enhance our view of the possibilities of humankind, to enlarge our perspective on what is best and finest from the past.

But of course such a general humanistic approach is not all that the material demands. On the face of it, Jeremiah came before his peers not as a thoughtful teacher from whom people could learn something but as a spokesman for Almighty God. Though a good many people evidently dismissed his claim or ignored it, other people just as obviously took it seriously and took his messengership to heart, particularly in the years that followed the tragedy of the fall of Jerusalem. And in the centuries that followed, the collected material about Jeremiah, together with similar material from other prophets, began to be laid alongside Deuteronomy and the other books of law and history that were being looked upon in the Jewish community as authoritative, as Scripture. When the Christian church, which grew out of the Jewish community, took over that body of Scripture, it continued to maintain the conviction that this was Scripture for the church as well.

So the kind of statement I have made so far—Jeremiah was convinced that God spoke through him to his people—is not enough. That is a statement about one person's belief at a time in the past; it is a *historical* statement, a verifiable statement—at least theoretically. Now it is important to see whether the second kind of statement—God speaks to us now through Jeremiah—is a meaningful way to speak. That is a *theological* statement, a statement of faith on our part; a statement of faith that God exists, that someone named Jeremiah heard God rightly, or at least rightly enough to be helpful to his peers and to later generations in their listening to God, and that we ourselves can hear God rightly enough through the material of Jeremiah to be able truly to respond to God. This kind of statement is of course not verifiable in the same way as the historical statement could be. "Faith is the assurance of things *hoped for*, the conviction of things *not seen*" (Heb. 11:1, italics added). The question of whether such a statement of faith is a useful way to talk is a far more complex problem than most of us have recognized. I say this in spite of the fact that in the Nicene Creed, one of the great traditional creeds of the Christian church, one of the sentences reads, "He [God the Holy Spirit] has spoken through the prophets." What might it mean for us to affirm that God has spoken to us through Jeremiah?

Plainly, Jeremiah was a part of a very particular and unique historical situation. In his time the fall of Jerusalem loomed and then actually happened. A specific government had been in specific difficulties and then had disappeared. These circumstances prevailed once and will never recur. In what way, then, do later generations have any justification for lifting Jeremiah's story out of its original matrix and making it their own, for their own particular and unique times? For this is what later generations have done. One of my colleagues, Phyllis Trible, describes this process:

All scripture is a pilgrim, wandering through history, engaging in new settings, and ever refusing to be locked in the box of the past.[1]

How might we hear God authentically when we do this? Jeremiah himself, so far as the evidence goes, had no eye for the far future, our future. His eye was on his own near future, a future in the hand of God that grew directly out of the choices that his own people were making as he spoke. How are we justified, then, in casting Jeremiah adrift from his mooring in the seventh and sixth centuries B.C.E. and allowing him to lodge in our present? If we do this, is he still recognizably Jeremiah? Can we hear God in this process? If so, how?

The first temptation, when hearing the prophets' words of passion for justice and their appeal for repentance, is to apply their words directly to our own public situation. Thus if Jeremiah condemned King Jehoiakim for being insensitive to the will of God, one might conclude that his words may be applied directly to the head of our government, a president of the United States, for example. But this is too simple. For one thing, from the point of view of political power the kingdom of Judah is not at all comparable to the United States of America. Judah was a small state threatened by large imperial powers, while the United States is one of the great powers of the present day.

Further, theologically the two are not comparable. Judah understood itself to be the sole surviving portion of the people of God called "Israel," called to be God's blessed community in the world, a demonstration to the world of what community should be. Judah understood itself thereby to stand under both the special judgment and special grace of God. Two verses from the book of Amos put it neatly:

> Hear this word that the Lord has spoken against you, O people of Israel, against the whole family which I brought up out of the land of Egypt: "You only have I known of all the families of the earth; therefore I will punish you for all your iniquities." (Amos 3:1–2)

But the United States, or any comparable modern nation-state, is hardly in the same position. It is true that the rhetoric of the early days of the American republic took its cue from biblical images: the Atlantic Ocean was comparable to the Jordan River, and the settlers often saw themselves as entering the promised land. But as the history of the United States unfolded, it became evident that such exclusive claims were not called for. Abraham Lincoln, in a speech he delivered before his first term of office as president, ironically referred to the people of the United States as "God's almost chosen people."[2]

The nature of the questions summed up by the words "church" and "state" are altogether different for us. "Law" for Jeremiah was law sponsored by God; "law" for us in a modern nation-state is law guaranteed by a secular constitution. The career of Martin Luther King, Jr., whom many people consider to be a modern "prophet," may illuminate the matter. He arose out of his church context and led the struggle for human rights for American blacks (and thus for everyone) in the context not only of God's justice but of that justice affirmed in American constitutional law. Thus he perceived (and we perceive) God to work in complex ways, through *both* the faith communities *and* the secular nation-state.[3]

But it must be stressed that when we speak today of the "people of God," we are not thinking (or should not be) of a single nation-state, as Judah did; instead, we think of the Jewish community, the Christian community, perhaps other communities, that cut across national lines. Therefore the words that Jeremiah addressed to the king of Judah, no matter how striking and pungent they may be, cannot be applied directly to any national leader today. If, for instance, the United States of America has sinned (and it has, of course—as all persons and political groups have sinned), one cannot expect the president of the United States to represent the American people in confessing the sin of the nation and asking the forgiveness of God. One might hope for an admission of wrongdoing on behalf of the American people but not for *repentance on behalf of the people.* That is not his job. It is, rather, the calling of various religious leaders on behalf of their respective communities, and indeed on behalf of all of us. The president's primary mandate is not to be the head of the people of God but rather the elected executive under the secular Constitution.

In short, our understanding today about how God works, through which groups and people God works directly, and through which groups and people God works indirectly is very different from what was assumed in Jeremiah's day. And, above all, the understanding of Christian communities is shaped by the intervening material of the New Testament, so that though we may have a keen sense that Jeremiah's words from God are *applicable,* we may not be able to say very directly *how* they are applicable. And the specific crucial problem is raised by that intervening material of the New Testament. A moment ago I cited the sentence from the Nicene Creed, "He [God in the Holy Spirit] has spoken through the prophets." But we may lay alongside that the opening words of the epistle to the Hebrews,

> In many and various ways God spoke of old to our fathers by the prophets; but in these last days he has spoken to us by a Son. (Heb. 1:1–2)

How do we handle that *contrast* between the way God spoke of old and the way God has spoken to the Christian community? Do we understand the Old Testament message to be *replaced* by the New Testament message? Or *supplemented* by the New Testament message? Or *explained* by the New Testament message? If the Old Testament message is replaced by the message of the New, then the Old Testament message, including Jeremiah, is really irrelevant except as a kind of curious and defective preliminary trial run. On the other hand, if the Old Testament is explained by the New, how are the contrasts between the Testaments to be understood?

We are in a tangle of issues here. So let us back away and examine several related parables to see if we can gain some clarity. The first parable is suggested by a remark made by Oscar Cullmann many years ago in his book, *Christ and Time:*

> *The decisive bottle in a war may already have occurred in a relatively early stage of the war, and yet the war still continues.* Although the decisive effect of that battle is perhaps not recognized by all, it nevertheless already means victory. But the war must still be carried on for an undefined time, until "Victory Day."[4]

He is suggesting by this illustration the situation of the Christian, whether of the mid-first century or the twentieth, who is living between the times: the decisive battle (Christ's defeat of Satan) has already occurred, though the victory (God's kingship) is not yet apparent to everyone.

To extend Cullmann's illustration slightly, imagine a crowd gathered underneath the balcony of the royal palace in a kingdom. A spokesman suddenly appears on the balcony. He has great news, he says; the cruel old king has been dethroned and imprisoned, and revolutionaries are about to declare a republic. And in this civil war the spokesman appeals to the crowd for support, food, arms, so that the struggle may continue and be crowned with success. A choice is now before each man, woman, child in the crowd: to trust the self-proclaimed spokesman on the balcony or not. Is he telling the truth? Or is he perhaps a madman? Or (a terrible possibility) is he an *agent provocateur* of the cunning old king, a king still thoroughly in control, who seeks by this trick to entrap some of his subjects into declaring themselves against him, so that he may rid himself of any opposition? This, I might suggest, is the choice we face as we listen to the appeal of the New

Testament, to its call to decision. The validity of the news from the spokesman on the balcony cannot be proved.

But our situation with an Old Testament spokesman like Jeremiah is still more complex and may be illustrated by a further extension of the parable. Imagine another scene, some years before the scene on the balcony. The king is cruel to his kingdom, and some of his subjects have begun to wonder whether they will ever be delivered from his rule. A day comes when several of the king's subjects idly turn the knob of a shortwave radio receiver. They accidentally pick up a broadcast from a neighboring state. Now that neighboring state has no cruel king but instead something perhaps even worse, a military dictatorship ruling through a secret police. This police state is blessed (if that is the word) by a technology beyond the dreams of the simple agrarian economy of the kingdom to which our radio listeners belong. And what is the news on the radio?

It is hard for our listeners to make out; their knowledge of the alien language is imperfect, and the static, alas, is heavy. But as far as they can tell, it is a clandestine broadcast—offering the news that a revolt of the people is under way, that both the dictator and the head of the secret police are under arrest. Again, as in our earlier parable, an appeal is broadcast for support from the population. What are our radio listeners to make of this? First they wonder whether they have heard and understood rightly. And then, assuming they have, they find the same kind of questions crowding into their minds as in the previous story: Is the report genuine, or the deed of a madman, or the clear work of an *agent provocateur*? But the situation is of course more complicated now, because this is not a revolution that directly concerns the kingdom to which our listener belongs, at least not yet. So still further questions arise in their minds: If the revolution is genuine, will it help or hinder our own situation? Can we gain help from them for our own struggle, or are our own circumstances so different as to make their struggle meaningless to us? What guidance, if any, can we gain from the static-ridden broadcast signal that we have just heard?

Here, then, is an analogy to our situation with an Old Testament prophet, a picture of the distance between ourselves and the Old

Testament material. To a certain degree we *are* eavesdroppers on the old conversation between God and God's people that took place in Jeremiah's lifetime. So how are we to handle the question?

I have titled this chapter "Prophet Out of Time," and by the title I want to suggest three things: (1) Jeremiah was indeed a prophet for God in his own time; (2) he speaks for God out of his own time into ours, and therefore serves as a means by which we may hear God; and (3) in a curious way he may even be said to be *more* at home in our time than in his own.

I shall not attempt here to justify an affirmation of the reality of God, or an affirmation of the reality of God's dealings with humankind in much the way the biblical material sets forth, specifically in the way the people of Israel envisaged God and the dealings of God with them. There is no way to prove the validity of the Old Testament witness about God, and I suppose that an agnostic might well make some sense out of the story of Jeremiah as an expression of aberrant psychology (whereby both the "God said" and "I said" of Jeremiah's expression could be understood as contrasting aspects of Jeremiah's conscious mind). The believing communities of Jews and Christians have deemed it eminently worthwhile to accept the validity, the reality, of the vision of Jeremiah and others in his tradition, and I build on that acceptance.

At the same time I hasten to affirm how keenly aware we must be of the symbolic nature of any talk about God. Thus saying "God is a person" really says that "person" is a more helpful, more adequate metaphoric description of God than any alternative (than saying, e.g., "God is a process"). So to say that Jeremiah's dialogues with that personal God represent a right perception of what is real about God is a highly symbolic way to talk. The Old Testament tradition, however, was just as aware as we are of how inadequate words are to deal with the reality of God. For example, in the first chapter of Ezekiel, the prophet attempts to describe the vision he has had of the throne-chariot of God, and after an elaborate and picturesque description, he concludes, "*Such* was the *appearance* of the *likeness* of the *glory* of the Lord" (Ezek. 1:28, italics added). Ezekiel is saying, Anything I can say to describe God is a good four steps removed from reality. With the caution, then, that any talk about God must inevitably be symbolic talk, we can affirm that Jeremiah was not mistaken, or demented, in his claim. He was not a false prophet. He really did speak for God in his generation.

By the same token we can affirm—and again without too much ado—that Jeremiah is a prophet "out of time," out of his own time into ours. And I do not say this simply because Jeremiah's story is now "in the book," that is, is now Scripture, or because the church or our own tradition tells us that we must believe the story to be relevant to us or truth to us. These are, in their way, possible reasons for affirming the speech of God to us through Jeremiah, but there are, I think, better reasons. We do not say it even because the story may fascinate us and fascinate others to whom the story has been introduced, though that is true too. Similar affirmations could be made about the stories of Socrates or Joan of Arc or Gandhi. No, we say it because we can gain through the story of Jeremiah an awareness of being addressed, of being caught up and dealt with in a way that both "breaks down" and "builds," both "plucks up" and "plants," to use once more the terms of Jeremiah's call. We sense that we may become transformed and our faith communities transformed by material like this. This is *why* it has become Scripture for the Jewish and Christian communities. It has not become Scripture because some synod or council said so; it has become Scripture because Jeremiah's experience of God's word as "fire" (23:29) continued to be the experience of others as they were exposed to that word. And in this experience we ourselves may share.

This experience continues to be valid even as it comes to us from before the New Testament experience. Thus we have seen how Jesus reinforces the word of Jeremiah that the Temple has become a "den of robbers," and we have sensed, too, how Jeremiah's inner experience with God may give us clues to Jesus' experience with God. Jesus would have affirmed God's words of judgment on Israel for breaking covenant that were delivered by Jeremiah, and he brooded over the suffering endured by prophets like Jeremiah ("O Jerusalem, Jerusalem, killing the prophets and stoning those who are sent to you! How often would I have gathered your children together as a hen gathers her brood under her wings, and you would not!" [Luke 13:34]). Clearly Jesus lived out a different attitude toward his enemies than Jeremiah did, but this does not mean that we bypass Jeremiah, any more than Jesus did.

A Prophet Especially for Today

The title of this chapter may be understood in another sense: Jeremiah speaks not only from his time into ours, but he may speak to us in an even *more* special and direct way than he did *to his own time.* Sometimes we say that a remark is "out of character" or a picture is "out of focus." I suggest that Jeremiah, the prophet for God in his own day, was "out of time" in *this* sense, out of step with his own generation and more in step with ours. This is a new notion, one that takes a bit of discussion. How could Jeremiah be more at home with us than with his own generation? This is a strange suggestion, if there is any truth to the parable about eavesdropping that I offered a moment ago, if there is truth to our steady affirmation that Jeremiah was not conscious of the far future at all.

I am not, of course, suggesting that he deliberately spoke to the far future. No person in history ever has the understanding of his or her own place in history that later times can gain. I am not suggesting that Jeremiah looked to the far future, but rather that he was lonely in his own day for kindred spirits, and that our own generation offers such kindred spirits for him; that there may be ways in which we hear him, and thus hear God through him, more directly than his peers did. Thus I am not suggesting that Jeremiah deliberately spoke to the far future, but that God can speak to us in our context more directly than was possible, perhaps, to the people in Jeremiah's day through those words that Jeremiah spoke.

In what ways might Jeremiah speak to us more than to his own people? The first is in a way that I fear can only be measured subjectively. We gain the impression, as we become acquainted with Jeremiah in word and deed, that he was a person of great poetic skill, a person of innovativeness and daring in his mode of expression, a person of a highly original turn of mind. This impression is hard to illustrate concretely, particularly if we are confined to reading an English translation of the material, since much of the marvel and magic of a poem is lost in translation; the poetry of the Old Testament is no different in this regard. Jeremiah's innovativeness in poetic technique, then, is hard to measure, but in such discussions as the one we had of 4:23–26 (see chap. VII) we can at least gain some appreciation of his stature as a poet.

But then the question emerges more broadly: How, over the long distance of the centuries and the contrast of cultures, are we to measure "the originality of a mind," whatever that is? But still, subliminally perhaps, the impression comes from Jeremiah's words and works of an innovator, an independent thinker. That is a trait that appeals to many of us, possibly more than it may have appealed to his peers. This trait gives us warrant not to squelch any independent and innovative impulses in our own thinking and talking about God and God's work. Jeremiah's striking visions of the female embracing the man (31:22) and of the new covenant to be drawn up by God (31:31–34; see chap. X) embody the trait I am talking about.

In pondering the turn of Jeremiah's mind it is well to consider his use of irony. While irony appears throughout the Old Testament,[5] especially in the prophets, Jeremiah was a supreme ironist. It is ironic that the covenant people have abandoned their only real source of metaphorical water, namely, Yahweh, and that, then, because they must have water, they go after false sources of fertility, the Baals, digging metaphorical cisterns that do not produce water but simply hold water—except that in this case the cisterns leak. The Baals thus are not positive sources of fertility at all, they are negative, drawing off fertility (2:13; see chap. IV). It is ironic that Jeremiah offers Scripture for the people to use—Hosea 10:12 and Deut. 10:16 (see Jer. 4:3–4 and the end of chap. IV)—but that the people quote instead a proverb to excuse themselves from responsibility and psalm verses to direct Yahweh's wrath on their enemy—Prov. 16:9; Psalms 6:1; 79:6–7 (so Jer. 10:23–25).

A second way in which Jeremiah may speak to us is in his description of his social isolation (see the discussion of 15:17 in chap. VIII). Social isolation, as I noted earlier, was much rarer in Old Testament times than it is today. In Jeremiah's case it was both exemplified and climaxed in his call to celibacy, a call unique in the Old Testament (see pp. 89–90). It was a gesture that rendered his whole life inconceivable to his fellows. This aberrant character trait, whatever its origin may have been psychologically, served in Jeremiah's own mind as the positive vehicle for a message from God.

But it did bring him isolation, terrible isolation.

Now it is certainly true that what was highly odd in Old Testament times is often commonplace today; our age is crowded with alienated, isolated people. A good many of these people are of course not alienated and isolated in any fashion that indicates health or helpfulness, as Jeremiah's does. But at the same time there are a good many other people in our day who are alienated and isolated for what do seem to be healthy reasons: to avoid smothering, hostile parental control, or a culture that thrives on violence and cruelty. These alienated people may well resonate with the sad, soaring lines of Jeremiah, and here is one place at which Jeremiah meets a modern need in quite a modern way.

Other points of view about Jeremiah's isolation are possible. It is arguable, for example, that it was unhealthy, or we might say that his stance was creative in his own day but unrelated to our own kinds of alienation, which might be destructive instead, might be leading us away from the kind of solidarity we ought to be building in our own society. While these are defensible alternative ways of understanding the issue, I think that what I have set forth is more likely: Jeremiah's own isolation helps to give resonance to at least some kinds of positive feelings of isolation in our own day.

Closely related to his social isolation is Jeremiah's exploration of the problem of God, the third way in which he may appeal to us more than he did to his own generation. Jeremiah's expressions of bitterness to God and his astonishing frankness are striking (see chaps. VIII and IX). Recall that Jeremiah alone, among the prophets of whom we have record, found his own relationship to God to be a problem. Amos, so far as we know, simply let his mouth speak the word from God; so did Hosea and Isaiah and the rest. The other prophets sensed the two-way struggle between God and the nation and saw themselves as the mouthpieces for God in voicing that side of that struggle. Jeremiah, of course, also saw that two-way struggle and likewise voiced God's side of the struggle. But for Jeremiah it became a three-way struggle; God, Jeremiah, and the people were all involved in the argumentation. God had a bill of complaints against the people, but Jeremiah for his part had a bill of complaints against God (see esp. chap. VIII). Jeremiah's perception offers an excitement to which many of us can respond. The Old Testament scholar Gerhard von Rad has put it well:

> [The confessions] all point alike to a darkness which the prophet was powerless to overcome, and this makes them a unity. It is a darkness so terrible—it could also be said that it is something so absolutely new in the dealings between Israel and her God—that it constitutes a menace to very much more than the life of a single man: God's whole way with Israel hereby threatens to end in some kind of metaphysical abyss. For the sufferings here set forth were not just the concern of the man Jeremiah, who here speaks, as it were, unofficially, as a private individual, about experiences common to all.[6]

Yes, and the narrow company of those who have embarked upon the exploration of despair before God as to God's ways—that company that began with Jeremiah and with the psalmist who sang, "My God, my God, why have you forsaken me?" and continued with Jesus, who repeated the psalm in his own hour of dereliction, through the medieval mystics who described the "dark night of the soul"—has become in our day a larger company, in a very different context, a context of rationalism, a context of doubt of all God-talk. It is a company of folk who cannot find the hand of God so clearly in the world and in their lives but who still, in the name of God, would question God's ways and struggle with God. And so to those people in that situation Jeremiah stands as a pioneer. What was an oddity in Jeremiah's time has become much more commonplace for us; and so here, as with his sense of isolation, he does seem more akin to us than to his own contemporaries.

So far, our answers to the question as to how Jeremiah speaks to us in our own day—his innovativeness, his eye for irony, his sense of social isolation, his seeing his relationship to God to be a problem—have focused on Jeremiah. But, since we are taking seriously his claim to be a *prophet,* we must ask what we may learn about *God* from Jeremiah.

Earlier in this chapter I indicated one approach that is too simplistic: to apply a word of Jeremiah's *directly* to a situation of our own that, at least superficially, seems parallel; my example was to expect a president of the United States to repent on behalf of the American people. But if this is wrong, it is equally wrong to swing too far in the other direction, that is, in the direction of generalities. It will not do, when trying to hear God through Jeremiah, to confine what we learn to statements like "God always wants people to be just and righteous" or "God expects us to be in solidarity with our neighbors." Such lessons can be gained from almost any page of Scripture, indeed, from almost any page of any other moral teacher across human history. To confine ourselves to such generalities is to trivialize the precious specificities of Jeremiah.

What then? There is another solution, one that is obvious but also radical and frightening to many of us. The purpose of all Scripture, ultimately, and certainly the purpose of the book of Jeremiah for us, is to lead us, by the hints in the book, to become acquainted with God for ourselves, to enter into our own dialogue with God. The great complaint in Jeremiah 2, we recall, is that the people had turned their back on God (see chap. IV). So, in our turn we are called to turn our face toward God, to enter into dialogue with God, become involved with God, allow God to show us how we are responsible for our common life.

This is obvious, I say, and yet frightening. We would far rather retreat into generalities—justice or solidarity or peace—than face the consequences of any obligation to become directly acquainted with God ourselves.

What the book of Jeremiah offers us, then, is a slice of God's dialogue with the covenant people (and with Jeremiah) at a particular time in history. By eavesdropping on this dialogue, we can become better acquainted with God and become enabled all the more securely to embark upon our own dialogue with God in our own day. The pages of the book of Jeremiah allow us specific instances of God's reaction to the life of the people of God. And since the lives of the Israelites, though in some ways so very different from our own, are at the same time in other crucial ways not so very different after all, we catch some of the clues we need to begin responding to God ourselves.

For example, we saw from the Temple Sermon (7:1–12) that God rejected the people's absolute trust in the Temple (see chap. III). This does not necessarily mean for us that God is against our own liturgies or the Vatican or the National Council of Churches or a particular television evangelist. But it does mean that God *can* reject our trust in our religious institutions, and did, once. How then does God react to our liturgies or to our various religious establishments? The book of Jeremiah urges us to find out.

God declared war on God's own people, according to the material in 4:5 and following (see chaps. V, VI, and VII). This should not mean automatically that God is against us today, but it might mean that God *can* be. The question then beckons: Do we perceive any ways in which God is against us, now? And such a question leads us all into situations of prayer and discussion that can become part of an ongoing dialogue of listening to God and speaking to God in our own day.

Perhaps the most striking impression we gain from eavesdropping on Jeremiah's presentation of God is the way God is portrayed as being innovative. That is what bothered Hananiah so (Jeremiah 28; see chap. IX). God is constantly changing the agenda. Of course this portrayal of God is not limited to Jeremiah; it is mediated through Isaiah (see Isa. 10:5–15), and through Jesus, for that matter (see Matt. 20:1–15). But it is peculiarly apparent in Jeremiah.

Some years ago the British scholar J. B. Phillips wrote a little book called *Your God Is Too Small.*[7] His title embodies Jeremiah's message as well: Your God is too small. You thought the God you worshiped needed the Temple and Zion and Jerusalem and kingship in the line of David and the army of Judah and all the rest. But you are wrong; God is far, far above all these specificities. God does not *need you*, or your religious system, or your notions of state and worship. God does not *need* the whole wide world, even; God is far beyond these little necessities. God is constantly considering new possibilities, bringing new patterns when the old ones have decayed, bringing new life where there has been only death. Open your ears and listen to God; shake yourself loose from the ways of the past. You can depend on nothing at all in this world, nothing at all in God, even, save one thing only: God's steady purpose and promise to the people.

The question posed to us in our own day, then, by this shaft of light from the past is very simple: Are we up to it? Are we up to such a vision of God which, if followed loyally, would mean a shaking loose from all conventional verities? Are we really up to it?

There is one more problem here, already touched on, of which we must take account, and that is this: Jesus interposes himself between Jeremiah and us. Has Jesus not given us his reassurance in the face of the yawning abyss of Jeremiah's view of God? To be more specific, has Jesus not reassured us that all is well between ourselves and God, so that we no longer need to be threatened by the possibility that God would declare war on the people? After all, Paul wrote:

> We know that in everything God works for good with those who love him, who are called according to his purpose. . . . What then shall we say to this? If God is for us, who is against us? . . . I am sure that neither death, nor life, nor angels, nor principalities, nor things present, nor things to come, nor powers, nor height, nor depth, nor anything else in all creation, will be able to separate us from the love of God in Christ Jesus our Lord. (Rom. 8:28, 31, 38–39)

Given *this* set of signals, what relevance can those earlier signals from Jeremiah possibly have for us? This is the same question as that asked earlier in this chapter, as to whether the New Testament replaces, supplements, or explains the Old Testament.

Our answer to this question depends somewhat on our taste and tradition. Many Christians, in view of the more hopeful perspective of the New Testament, will set aside the image of God's warfare upon God's own people as having a once-and-for-all relevance. In effect, then, they will assume that in this respect at least the New Testament does replace the Old.

Others, and I confess myself to be included here, are not so sure. Perhaps my own approach is exemplified by the statement, made many years ago, that the task of a newspaper is to comfort the afflicted and to afflict the comfortable. I sense that this was the task of anyone who spoke for God as well: to afflict the comfortable in times of plenty and complacency (as Jeremiah did before the fall of Jerusalem) and to comfort the afflicted in times of penury and dismay (as Jeremiah did at the time of the fall of Jerusalem).

People often need one set of messages under one set of conditions, another set of messages under another set of conditions. Some years ago I had occasion to offer the same series of class sessions on Jeremiah to members of two different church groups during the same period of time. The first was a church in a suburban area of Boston. This congregation shares some of the liveliest and most genuine worship services in which I have ever participated, and out of this congregation thirty or forty men and women came each week to study Jeremiah. The other group I taught emerged out of a cooperative venture of five neighboring churches of various denominations in an inner-city area near the Boston airport. I was not able to share in the Sunday worship of any of these people, but certainly the buildings in which they worshiped, lovingly cared for though they were, had become far too large and far too much in need of renovation for the resources of their congregations; and the budgets of several of them were subsidized by their denominations. The twenty-odd people who came to these class sessions were bewildered, baffled people who clung to their neighborhood but had little sense of being in control of their lives.

The contrast in reaction of the two groups to the story of Jeremiah could hardly have been greater. The suburban church immediately became engrossed in the material and began to raise all sorts of important questions: How does the prophet get his word? How can we be sure we know how to respond ourselves to the word? What present-day issues are clarified by this word from the past? The inner-city people, on the other hand, were largely mute. Defeated to begin with, they hardly had room in their lives for one more tragedy from the past, no matter whether it was "in the book" or not. And I kept asking myself, What am I doing here? Why am I not witnessing to the New Testament gospel to these quiet, puzzled people?

Because, you see, the basic focus of Jeremiah's message, at least at the beginning of his ministry, was this: You can change the texture of your common life together. Turn about, reform your ways with your neighbors, restore your vision of the common welfare, respond to God's call to justice and peace, and perhaps even now God will call off the foe from the north. But to listen on *this* wavelength implies a certain awareness of and belief in one's control over the life of one's community. And those who do have a certain measure of control over the life of their community and who do *not* hear the word from Jeremiah and respond to it have missed part of God's word for our day.

But the people in the inner city had felt largely trapped in their lives for years. They were only at the beginning stages of recovering any sense of even partial control over the life of their community. (One evening one of their pastors announced, "Tomorrow morning at nine o'clock there will be a public hearing at Faneuil Hall regarding the proposed extension of the runways of Logan Airport. I hope that as many of you as can will be there to show the solidarity on this matter which we all feel in this neighborhood.") These people sensed, deep down, that their lives had been ruled not by the modern equivalent of King Jehoiakim, who can be addressed by Jeremiah, but rather by the modern equivalent of principalities and powers (Rom. 8:38), whom no one can get at. What they desperately needed to hear was the story that once upon a time, once and for all, God signaled to us that these principalities and powers have no ultimate hold on our poor little lives, if only we quietly say yes to God.

Both messages we need; both messages we have. One does not cancel the other, for both of them come from the same God, a God who works within history and yet works beyond history, and in spite of history, as well.

So we expand the beachhead of Scripture with which we are familiar, moving out beyond the well-used passages of the gospels and epistles and psalms, to listen in on the prophets of old, who had a message for their time that was startling and shocking, a message that God expects us, too, to hear. And among these prophets, not the least is Jeremiah.

NOTES

1. Phyllis Trible, "Ancient Priests and Modern Polluters," *Andover Newton Quarterly* (November 1971): 75.

2. The phrase occurs in an address at Trenton, New Jersey, February 21, 1861.

3. See the eloquent essay by Martin Luther King, Jr., *Letter from Birmingham Jail* (Philadelphia: American Friends Service Committee, 1963), reprinted conveniently in *A Testament of Hope: The Essential Writings of Martin Luther King, Jr.*, ed. James M. Washington (San Francisco: Harper & Row, 1986), 289–302.

4. Oscar Cullmann, *Christ and Time* (Philadelphia: Westminster Press, 1950), 84. The italics are his.

5. For an unsystematic survey see Edwin M. Good, *Irony in the Old Testament* (London: SPCK, 1965; 2d ed., Sheffield: Almond Press, 1981).

6. Gerhard von Rad, *Old Testament Theology* (New York: Harper & Row, 1965), 2:204, reprinted in *The Message of the Prophets* (New York: Harper & Row, 1972), 173–74.

7. J. B. Phillips, *Your God Is Too Small* (New York: Macmillan Co., 1953).

SCRIPTURE INDEX

References in this index to substantial discussions of verses and longer passages in Jeremiah are *italicized*.

Old Testament

New Testament